Improspectives®

Improspectives®

Curtis D. Frye

Technology and Society, Inc.

Portland, Oregon

Cataloging-in-Publication data for this book is available from the Library of Congress.

First Technology and Society edition 2012

ISBN 978-0-9852709-0-2 (trade paperback)

ISBN 978-0-9852709-1-9 (e-book)

Table of Contents

Preface

Why *Improspectives*? Why write a book on improvisational comedy and business? Isn't there just one improv principle, the "Yes, and…" principle that applies to everything and solves every problem?

I hope my improv colleagues will forgive me for saying this, but the answer is "NO!" The "Yes, and…" principle, which states that performers should accept and add to whatever their fellow players say or do, is a terrific base for many personal interactions. The problem lies in the real conflicts of life, not the contrived conflicts of the stage.

The most basic improv skills are effective listening and clear communication. As the world adopts a faster pace and more agile development cycle, even technical specialists must learn to communicate effectively.

ON THE FASTRACK © 2011 KING FEATURES SYNDICATE

Gaining these abilities lies at the heart of the Improspectives approach. After reading this book, you will be better prepared to take on challenges in the personal and business facets of your life. As you gain skill and confidence, you will apply these principles effectively and learn even more as you go. All you need to do is to get started.

1

What Is Improv?

Improvisation, usually shortened to *improv*, is an unscripted theatrical production. In its purest form, improv entails one or more individuals going on stage and creating a performance with no pre-planning. Most audiences find pure improv to be unrewarding because there's no sense of play – there's no way to prove that what you're seeing on stage wasn't actually scripted.

The next level is when the performers take a suggestion from the audience and build their scene or presentation from that single suggestion. Performers can also take multiple suggestions and build all or most of them into the scene, or perhaps take a bunch of suggestions and select them at random to guide the scene as it goes along. This form of improv provides deeper audience interaction. Many performers find it more challenging because it helps them get away from their preconceived notions and avoid repeating actions from previous scenes or shows.

There are two main types of improvisational comedy. The first type is *short form*, which consists of a series of scenes or games between 3 to 5 minutes in length. The scenes and games are over quickly so the audience is constantly engaged, plus the actors have room to get many more suggestions. *Long form* improv, by contrast, generally involves performances of least 20 minutes, and either spring from a single suggestion from which a series of interrelated scenes are created, or from a series of suggestions that are all incorporated into the show.

At the fringe of the genre is *sketch-prov*, which is where the improvisers have a prepared outline and build the audience's suggestions into the scene. For example, you might have a scene set in a doctor's office, ask for a type of doctor, and then incorporate the suggestion into your format.

Finally, you can just fake it. That's where the performers ask for suggestions, pretend to hear the one they want, and perform scripted scenes based on the phantom suggestions.

Standup comedy is not really improv unless the performers happen to forget what they were going to say, or if they come up with a new line based on their interaction with the audience. On the professional level, standup comedy is almost always entirely scripted and well-rehearsed. Standup is extremely demanding, in some ways more so than improv, because the audience knows what they are seeing was prepared and therefore have higher expectations.

In many ways, improv is a very forgiving art form. The audience understands that what they're seeing is being made up on the spot, so they're willing to forgive inconsistencies in plot, song lyrics, character naming, and other aspects that otherwise would interrupt the flow of a performance that they knew to be scripted. Also, the audience gets immediate feedback in improv. Whenever the performers use or incorporate a suggestion into the act, the audience understands that the performers are listening to them and honoring their input. That's a powerful gift no performer should take for granted.

So how does improv relate to everyday life? Well, I certainly didn't wake up this morning with a script of what was going to happen, so that means that I've been making things up the entire time that I've been awake. There's a huge difference between improvising your way through life and making it entertaining. Most humans thrive on their daily routine, so very few of us go through life completely making up what it is we're going to do next. Rather than entirely making things up as we go along, we adhere to something akin to a social contract. This contract states that we are going to stay on the path everyone expects, with only minimal deviations, unless we all accept that those changes are permissible.

The Improv State of Mind

What makes up the improv state of mind? If I had to break it down into a list of qualities, I'd include the following:

- Maintaining a high level of controlled energy

- Listening and attending to everything said

- Possessing a willingness to change course immediately

- Trusting your fellow improvisers

- Knowing when the scene is over

Maintaining a high energy level, not just the appearance of a high energy level, almost goes without saying. Yes, there are many improvisers who can perform quite respectably while tired, far fewer who can give an interesting performance while intoxicated, and one in a million who can be interesting to anyone except themselves while practicing freelance pharmacology. Unless the audience is high, too – then they'll laugh at anything.

You must listen. It's impossible to have an improv scene if you don't pay attention to what your fellow players are saying and doing. It's perfectly acceptable to have a completely silent scene, but then you must pay careful attention to every nuance of your fellow performers' actions and intention. By assigning importance to what your fellow players say and do, you allow what they say to affect you.

A willingness to let what your fellow performers say and do affect you is what lets you change course immediately. Any time you are in a scene, or perhaps a meeting, you are only partially in control. You can certainly choose to steamroll through your colleagues' reactions, but you will often find that it makes more sense to acknowledge what was said or done and to let it affect you. You might also find that a decision you made, or actions you planned, don't fit with new data that has been introduced during your presentation. If that's the case, you need to adapt.

Trust is vital to any successful transaction, whether on stage or in business. Trust is earned over time. It's entirely possible to have an effective team with less than perfect trust between the members, but the psychic cost of those interactions grows with time. These pressures often cause improv groups to implode, and can cost businesses some of their best contributors if they are willing and able to take their talents to another company or team with a less toxic environment.

The last element, knowing when a scene is over, is a skill that many improvisers struggle with throughout their careers. Technical specialists aren't always skilled at reading body language, and many of them have tested the patience of hundreds of individuals over the years. It's also difficult to know when a discussion is effectively over in business; that once a decision has been made and instructions have been given to move forward, it's time to let things go. Businesses must move forward to provide value for their shareholders, which can't be done if you constantly rehash positions and plans.

Even though we don't spend all our time in a pure improvisational state, using improv techniques can help you get through life and your business dealings. Those techniques include listening, accepting all offers, limiting denials, limiting questions, and taking responsibility for forwarding the scene. Improvisers use these techniques to ensure that the product they produce is worth watching, and satisfies both audience and performer. The last thing any performer wants is to get in a rut. That means you need to find variety and branch out occasionally so you're not limited to one form of performance.

Improv in the Business World

Improv, which is really a form of play, might not seem to fit into the world of serious business. I disagree. There are plenty of times when you don't want to try to be funny, but that doesn't mean that you shouldn't approach situations with a playful outlook. As Michael Schrage says in the 1999 Harvard Business School Press book *Serious Play*:

> The irony of innovation in any field — especially in markets wracked by intensifying competition — is that you can't be a serious innovator unless you're willing and able to play. Consequently, serious play shouldn't be treated as either management metaphor or word game. Serious play is both the practice and perspective on what makes innovation possible. Practically everyone who's been a child knows what it means to play to win,

to play for fun, and to play to discover.

In the rest of this book, I'll discuss preparing to improv; playing characters; listening, processing, and reacting to offers made during a scene or conversation; playing the games within the games; building an effective team; and creating and evaluating improv performances. Then, I'll show you in detail how I drew great value from a book written by a non-improviser. After a few closing thoughts, you'll find an Appendix with a series of improv games you can play to help your groups warm up and play together. Take it easy at first—improv isn't something you can take to the limit immediately. When everyone starts having fun, you might find they're interested in continuing, inventing their own rules, and perhaps even creating their own games.

2

Getting Ready to Improv

In the previous chapter, I mentioned several aspects of successful improvisers. Basically, you are looking for a playful energy and a willingness to accept what your teammates bring to the table. Yes, you will have to adjust as the scene goes along, but that is an extremely small price to pay when your audience is entertained.

Letting Go

One hard lesson in improv is learning how to relax the urge to control everything. Some players never learn how to let things go. For them, we have a joke:

> *Me: Knock, knock.*

> *You: Who's there?*

> *Me: Control freak. Now you say, "Control freak who?"*

Players who are overly controlling rarely rise very high in the improv world. Most of the time, these individuals need to start their own improv troupe to progress. In many ways, being in charge is the best place for them. There is the question, of course, of how well they work with other improvisers, each of whom has individual ideas, but that is more question of how their management style meshes with the players they bring in.

Hiring is an art form, one that is extremely difficult and dependent upon your organization, its culture, your team, and the skill set required for the open position. I said it's an art, but in many ways it's a dark art. You're going on intuition and hoping everything on the applicant's resume is reasonably accurate. You might have numerous qualified candidates to choose from. I wish I had some good advice, but the best that I can tell you is to rely on your intuition and to learn from the hiring managers in your organization. Learning which questions they ask, and what they look for in a successful applicant, will help you find individuals who can thrive in their role and succeed with your company.

Warming Up

In my improv group, we spend a fair amount of time before each show going through some warm-ups. The goal is to start working together, thinking together, and getting our energy up. We always play a variety of games within the show, so we do our best to warm up in a way that gives us a flexible set of tools to use during the performance.

Some of the best warm-ups are extremely simple, and, in many cases, are college drinking games. One of my favorite warm-ups is called Zip-Zap-Zop. The game goes like this: Everyone stands in a circle, and someone leads off by pointing at another player and saying *zip*. That player points at another player and says *zap*. The player just pointed out points to yet another player (repeats are allowed) and says *zop*. You play this game until someone makes a mistake. You can mess up by not responding quickly enough when you're pointed to, saying the wrong word, or responding when someone else was pointed to.

The trick to making this game an effective warm-up is to start at a reasonable pace and speed up after everyone has responded a few times. If you're not playing fast enough to mess up, you need to speed up. If you want, you can add variations to adjust the difficulty of the game. You might allow repeats that are established after the first player says *zip*. For example, the first player says *zip* and points at another player. That second player can either say *zap* as in the normal game or say *zip* again. If the second player said *zip* as well, the third player can either say a third *zip* or a *zap*. Let's say the third player says *zap*, which means that there is a pattern established of two *zips*. In this version of the game, we need to have two of everything: there were two *zips*, so we need two *zaps* and two *zops*.

If you want to make the game incredibly difficult, you can have everyone shift in position around the circle. Let's say that you start in position one. You play the game until someone messes up. When that happens, everyone shifts one spot to the right, but your improviser essence remains in your original position. Whenever someone points to your original position, regardless of the player occupying that space, you must respond. You keep playing and shifting every time someone messes up until you reach your original position. It's a fun game for an advanced group to play, but I don't recommend trying it the first couple of times you attempt Zip-Zap-Zop.

I like to warm up during my business day by answering routine e-mail. I don't want to have to do any serious thinking the instant I stagger sleepily to my desk, but I can answer straightforward questions reasonably well. Once the easy stuff is done, I can turn to more challenging tasks and hopefully complete everything in a reasonable time so I can begin new work for the day.

When you work in an office, don't forget to warm up as a

team. That could mean saying hello to coworkers as you get coffee, starting the day with a rousing planning meeting, or just waving at folks as you walk to your desk. Regardless of how you do it, you should always take time to connect, even if briefly, with your coworkers. Being part of the team is important, and renewing those contacts frequently helps you communicate effectively when you need to solve a problem together.

These morning warm-up conversations rely on relationship listening, which I discuss in more detail in Chapter 4: Listening, Processing, and Reacting.

The Power of the Suggestion

Every improv group is different, so I don't need to go into too much detail about how to set up a show, but most groups have an introduction that lets everyone know what is going to happen and how the audience members will participate.

One of the best ways to have audience members participate in an improv show is to let them give suggestions. You could almost argue that audience interaction is what defines improv. After all, if the audience didn't have any input into the show, you might as well write something and perform it as sketch comedy.

After you've done a few hundred shows, you will probably become weary of the most common suggestions. In fact, one of the arts of improv is finding ways to ask for suggestions so you get new responses. You do this for several reasons. If you offer your own suggestion, meaning that you start improvising based on something you thought of before the show, the audience won't believe that it is improv; they'll think you're just doing a sketch. Another problem with suggestions is that you can go *fishing*. You are fishing when you ask for a suggestion in a category, such as an occupation, and then you wait until you get the one you want.

For example, if you were to ask for an occupation that involves physical labor, audience members could shout out jobs such as bricklayer, mason, or plumber. If what you're going for is lumberjack you can say "Yes, that's a good suggestion…what else?" until someone says lumberjack. You're cheating, and the audience knows it.

In some ways, fishing is worse than simply doing a scene based on your own suggestion. Fishing teaches your audience that you will keep asking until you hear exactly what you want. If you are really improvising, and basing your work on their suggestions, you should take whatever you hear first. Most of the moderators in improv comedy groups ensure that whatever suggestion they hear first is what they take. Some groups, who approve of fishing, use it to ensure that the suggestion is the right quality to include in a scene.

I hope I don't have to convince you that judging which suggestions are good quality and which aren't insults the audience. If you're only prepared to do scenes about a particular occupation or set of occupations, you are not doing improv. More importantly, you are not honoring the audience.

At the extreme, you could have a group whose moderator asks for a suggestion in a particular category and pretends to hear the answer they wanted. This exact scenario happened in Dallas. A friend of mine from ComedySportz Portland went to Dallas for a conference. While he was there, he went to a show put on by an "improv" group that will remain nameless. He enjoyed it so much that he went back the next night, and saw exactly the same show.

Suggestions in Business

Let's look at suggestions in a business context. There will be plenty of times when you walk into a situation and know exactly what is going on. Everything will conform to your expectations and you will solve the problem quickly. On the other hand, you might look into the situation and need your customer's feedback so you can start to solve the problem. If that's the case, you need to know how to ask questions to get the information you require. These facts are the suggestions you use to start your business "scene." Most customers are not experts, even the ones who think otherwise. You need multiple ways of asking for information. You can ask simple questions such as "When did the computer start behaving this way?" or "Did you install any new software before the computer started acting strangely?" These tactics let you discover the information that you need to begin your work.

When you're doing an improv show, you're less worried about getting the right result and much more concerned about producing a result that entertains the audience and satisfies you as a player. I have lost count of the number of scenes I've done about monkeys, or the times another player has replaced my softball bat with a banana in guessing games.

The trick to staying fresh with improv, while honoring your audience's suggestions, is to find new ways to ask for items in well-worn categories. You could ask for an animal that doesn't start with a, l, or z. Sorry, no aardvarks, lions, or zebras. We get those a lot. After the film *Napoleon Dynamite* came out, we got liger every hour on the hour for several weeks. If you want something completely new, you might ask for a weather phenomenon or perhaps a new word the audience learned in the last month.

As you continue on in your work, you should find new ways to get information, while keeping the process interesting. The more tools you have your disposal to acquire information, the better your work experience will be.

How to Be Bad at Improv

As with most professions, there are many more ways to be bad at improv than there are to be good. Fortunately, improv is a very forgiving art form. If you perform with the right colleagues, you can succeed as long as you keep the needs of your fellow performers and your audience in mind. That said, there are some surefire ways to make your scenes less than successful.

One of the easiest ways to take the air out of the scene is to say "no." As an example, consider the following exchange:

Player 1: Steve, that's a beautiful sweater you're wearing.

Player 2: It's not a sweater; it's a Polo shirt.

Player 1: You're right; I need to get my glasses cleaned.

Player 2: You're not wearing glasses.

What has happened? Absolutely nothing. By denying, or saying no, the respondent in the previous scene completely blocked any possibility of progress.

Another way to be bad at improv is to go for the joke. Selfish improvisers often try to make themselves look good at any cost, even if means immediately derailing a scene. Here's an example:

Player 1: Steve, that's a beautiful sweater you're wearing.

Player 2: That's what she said!

What happened? Absolutely nothing. By going for the joke, the second player has completely stopped the momentum of the scene. Worse, the players probably made themselves look foolish because most members of the audience have heard that line before. It has become a cliché.

Still another way to be bad at improv is to micromanage every aspect of the scene and not give the other players a chance to influence the outcome. In my early days as an improviser, I made one such faux pas during a Shakespeare game when our suggestion was bicycle racing:

Me: Indeed, good Campagnolo, I have been on the Suntour, where I have seen the sprockets of Fuji and now wear the world champion's rainbow vest.

Him: Thou hast taken all the good references!

I deserved that.

Micromanaging is a difficult habit to escape. Whenever a scene partner takes things in an unexpected direction, micromanagers are prone to trying to nudge things back, sometimes in less than subtle ways. These attempts to influence the scene result in some of the most passive-aggressive denials you've ever seen. They are annoying and disrupt the audience's enjoyment of the scene. At worst, they anger the other players and ruin everyone's evening.

When a player makes an odd reference to something, like an alien culture, light sabers, or something that smells of pixie dust or glitter, we call it "going to the moon." It's often a weak choice, little more than a chance to get wacky and have the audience laugh at something unusual. The problem is that you lose one of the fundamental advantages of improv: a connection to the audience members' personal experiences. The more what you do reminds your audience of their lives, the more they will like you, the more they will identify with you, and the more they will appreciate what you're doing.

Once you've established that connection, you can make a subtle twist, perhaps by doing something unexpected in an office place. It's fun to pull a coffee pot from a file drawer! The audience will laugh because it is both an unexpected twist and something they can identify with.

Another good way to do bad improv is to be disconnected from your fellow players. There will be times when a performer can be on stage doing things that don't contribute directly to the scene, but provide an atmosphere that enhances the audience's experience. Most players who do this want to bring attention to themselves. We call this "pulling focus" because it distracts the audience from the legitimate focus of the scene.

Even if you're not an improviser, I'm sure you've encountered individuals in your everyday and business lives who use the same sort of tricks to gain attention, to fight for control, or to block progress because things aren't going the way they want.

How do you deal with people like this? In most cases, at least in improv, their reactions and behaviors are due to low self-confidence and, frankly, inexperience. These individuals want to be good improvisers and function as part of the group. The best way to deal with them is through side coaching during workshops and through notes after shows. It's even better if you can record your shows so you have video evidence of what happened. You can have the same effect by taking accurate minutes during a meeting. In the business world, you can address the problem through peer feedback and coaching from the individual's manager or skip-level manager.

Product vs. Process

Like anything worth doing, improvisation is easy to do but difficult to master. One way to manage the complexity is to introduce a process. One of the earlier forms of improvisation was the sixteenth-century Italian *commedia dell'arte*. *Commedia* has a set of well-defined characters with associated bits, called *lazzi*. For example, the Doctor is extremely vain and always knows everything about everything, even if he doesn't. Mezzetino serves wine at his master's dinner, but always drinks the wine before he pours it into anyone's glass. When the bottle is empty, he feigns surprise, acting as if he accidentally brought out an empty bottle, and runs to the pantry for another. Repeat as needed, or until it's not funny.

Generally with a *lazzo*, when a player initiates one of them, the other players immediately recognize what's going on and jump in to play their roles. An experienced troupe can have hundreds of *lazzi* available to them. The fool and trickster characters, such as Harlequin, would have many more *lazzi* in their repertoire than the other players. Even so, everyone has a role to play, and it was the duty of everyone to say "yes" when one of their fellow performers made an offer to go in a given direction.

Commedia dell'arte is still practiced throughout the world, though it's not as common as it once was. We still have stock characters that date back to time immemorial, such as the corrupt politician, the philandering lover, and the incompetent doctor, but in an age of 24-hour cable television, even the hardiest *commedia* group will run out of bits in fairly short order.

The improv comedy tradition I work in can be credited in large part to Keith Johnstone, who was director of the Loose Moose Theatre in Calgary, Alberta, Canada. Keith is the author of two terrific books: *Impro* and *Impro for Storytellers*. He also created what he called Theatresports, a form that took improvisational exercises that he used in class and turned them into a competition between two teams. He granted permission for ComedySportz to use his general format; we are grateful for both his permission and for his contribution to our shared art form.

Keith's process is very theatrical. One of the most interesting chapters in *Impro* deals with mask work. When you put on a mask, you become that character, with all its virtues and vices. Your personality falls away and you become that character. It's very important that there be someone in charge who is able to say "stop!" and have everyone take off their masks. You never know when someone is going to get carried away. I do not recommend mask work for anyone attempting any sort of improvisational exercises in a business setting or among inexperienced performers. It is an advanced technique and one that should be saved for individuals who are emotionally ready.

In one *Harvard Business Review* case study, "What's Stifling the Creativity at CoolBurst?", two analysts commented on a disastrous teambuilding exercise described in the case. They said, "advanced paradigm-breaking techniques, such as the wishful thinking exercise they tried to use, can be too much for people who are new to such things – too much because they may require a great deal of patience in trying to generate practical solutions."

There is a time and place for everything. Keep an open mind, but be aware that humor might not be appropriate in your situation.

In the business world, organizations develop processes to help manage their workflow on both the technical and creative sides. Authors often have a specific creative process that they use. Some writers prefer to create an outline of what they're going to write, while others favor writing a draft and rewriting as necessary. In the end, the stories they produce look pretty much the same. They follow the same general progression, with some obvious exceptions that stand out because they are unusual but worked anyway.

On the technical side of things, a lot of new software development models have a grown up around the Web: software as a service, cloud computing, and so on. Rather than creating monolithic applications that are changed once every few years, web companies tend to put out an initial release and then build on them incrementally as new features are requested or imagined by the product team. Other companies, such as Microsoft, put out new versions of their Microsoft Windows or Microsoft Office software every two to three years. They supplement these programs with occasional updates to fix bugs that slipped through the beta testing process, patch security holes, and meet customer requests. The full version of the software must be tested against a wide range of machines and operating systems representing the millions of users who take advantage of those programs.

In the improv world, groups emphasize product and processes to varying degrees. Some groups are focused on the process, and are willing to take whatever product comes out as long as they work towards applying the process correctly. The process changes from group to group, structure to structure, and sometimes from day to day.

For me, the ultimate goal of any improvised theater is to entertain the audience. That means I can't focus exclusively on my process and must ensure the product that results from the process entertains the audience. I am a commercial artist: I like being paid for what I do. The more I entertain my audience, the more likely it is that I will be able to make a decent living as a performer. And, as a natural comedian, I prefer to hear my audience laugh.

3

Playing Characters

We all take on different personas to meet the needs of a situation: parent, friend, partner, employee, manager, or teammate. In the improv world, we take on a variety of characters to fit the current scene. I've played everything from spinster librarians in search of love to Aztec warriors in search of bitter chocolate.

Characters are necessary for any improv scene—the players need to interact for the scene to progress, after all. Even so, characters aren't the only aspect (or even the most important aspect) of every scene. Science fiction author Orson Scott Card writes that there are usually four elements to a story. He calls it his MICE quotient:

M is for *milieu*, which is the environment of the story.

I is for *idea*, which is the overarching concept behind the story.

C is for *character*.

E is for *event*.

For example, the milieu could be the focus of the story as it is in *Gulliver's Travels*, which is all about the exploration of Lilliput. An idea-based story would be something like William Gibson's novel *Neuromancer*, which was written to explore the impact of television on society. Character novels are focus on individuals and what happens to them. Event stories often focus some sort of calamity, such as *Lucifer's Hammer*, a

Larry Niven novel about a meteor set to strike the Earth. Every story has a certain percentage of each MICE element, but you can change the texture of your story by emphasizing one aspect over another.

I've always been something of an outlier when it comes to improv and playing characters, mainly because when I read something, I'm far more interested in the ideas than in the characters. My favorite author is William Gibson. In addition to *Neuromancer*, he wrote *Spook Country*, *Pattern Recognition*, and several other books. His work focuses on ideas, such as how fashion affects modern culture or, in the case of *Neuromancer* (which is one of the classic works of the cyberpunk subgenre), how television affects our lives. It was only after the rise of the Internet that the term *cyberspace*, which Gibson coined in a previous work, truly took off.

Many improv players want to take their career beyond the group that they start in. If you follow the natural progression, it's not hard to see that the easiest way to move forward is to create a memorable character. Sketch shows, such as *Saturday Night Live*, run scenes that spotlight characters established by the cast members. What you might not know is that many of those characters were developed by using improv. There's a process called "improv to sketch," in which performers start talking and acting like their characters. Soon, the characters take on a life of their own.

Once you have a character, you can put it into different situations, exaggerating those situations to create comedy. Without a doubt, improv scenes benefit from the inclusion of strong characters. When you're performing a short form scene, one that is usually three to eight minutes, it's very difficult to develop an idea. The difficulty with focusing exclusively on characters, especially extremely strong characters, in a short form improv game is that there is usually room for only one at a time in a given scene. That means one player takes on the leading role (it would be more accurate to say the dominant role), and everyone else provides fodder for that character. If you work in a group in which there is one extremely strong player, or one extremely assertive player who isn't willing to share, the other players can get forced out of the spotlight.

I explain what can happen in a group when players aren't willing to share in Chapter 5, "The Games Within the Games." I'm thinking specifically of the game of Chicken, in which two players force the action, start to compete instead of cooperate, and either give in or cause a disastrous collision. The problem is worse in improv scenes. When two players play Chicken, the audience sees the tension rise among the players and the piece turns into a slow-motion car wreck that might end up in flames.

A scene about a milieu can lead to some interesting exploration. For example, you could be in a strange city or even an alien planet. My good friend Amy Gray came up with an exercise called the "tricorder exercise." In the various incarnations of the TV show *Star Trek*, members of away teams always carried *tricorders*. Tricorders are universal analysis devices that gather information about the environment; any aliens the team encounters, and so on.

Amy's tricorder exercise involved a team beaming down to a planet and describing what they saw and what their tricorders picked up. The point of the exercise was to determine what was in the environment and then, once we knew what was there, to interact with it in interesting and (hopefully) funny ways.

Event scenes easier than idea scenes, mainly because there's something driving the action and the players have things to react to. One basic event game that you can play is called It Gets Worse. You can start by asking for a location. When I played with a group named Mprov in the Washington, DC area, we always seemed to start on a diving board. You then ask for three calamities. Almost every time we got diving board as the opening suggestion, the swimming pool would be out of water, the ladder would catch on fire, and the players would be out of toilet paper. It's interesting how our minds work.

Andrew Berkowitz came up with a two-person exercise for events: He gave us a simple task, such as combing our hair or buying milk, and then played the *Mission: Impossible 2000* theme song. Our job was to come up with obstacles preventing us from completing the task. The song runs 3 minutes and 17 seconds, so we had to pile on the obstacles during the first 100 seconds and overcome them during the last minute and a half.

Characters and Persona

You've probably encountered quite a few people who focus on being characters. For example, the person at a party who believes she is a raconteur, or perhaps the loner who stands in the corner reading a book of his own poetry. These individuals have a character in mind, and they use various tactics to generate the desired impression. We all do this to an extent. My personal character is someone who's more or less invisible; my standard costume is a black polo shirt, a pair of jeans, and Nike tennis shoes. I blend seamlessly into the Portland, Oregon scenery. I could be more invisible only if I were wearing flannel.

You can learn a lot about a person by studying the contrast between who he really is and the character he attempts to portray. Someone who's loud and assertive might be compensating for insecurities. Someone who comes across as quiet might just be waiting for the right moment to speak. The only way to know for certain is to observe the person. If you work with someone and you know that, given time, she can come up with wonderful ideas, play to her strengths! Set her up to win! These individuals are often very attentive to detail and consider many factors instead of just one or two before making a decision. If you're focusing on strategy or tactics for a situation and time isn't of the essence, this type of individual is extremely useful. You'll be happy to have her on your side because of her imagination and keen observations.

On the other hand, there are people, like me, who tend to process information rapidly and try to offer solutions early in the decision-making process. They are helpful because they rarely censor themselves. They generate ideas and offer them so they don't disappear in the cascade of thoughts. These individuals are extremely useful in brainstorming sessions, as long as you record the session, or have someone who can write quickly to capture the ideas. With these ideas, you'll have the raw materials you need to make decisions. It's very important that you do not judge ideas at this point. The hardest part in the planning process is staring at a blank page and wondering what you're going to do next. If you start talking and creating ideas, regardless of how outlandish they might seem, you'll have something to work from.

You can use character exercises to generate personas for your typical customers. You should design your products with those archetypes in mind.

Character in Context

As I said before, I'm quite a bit different from your standard improvisational comedy player. I play characters to an extent, but I'm much more concerned about honoring audience suggestions. I want to explore the audience's idea in its natural context, such as at a microchip engineering company or a law firm. I was reluctant to play characters for many years despite receiving multiple notes that I should work on doing more distinct characters. I resisted because, to me, it was the least interesting part of the show. I began to see myself as what I would call a "remote specialist." In our group, "remotes" are travel shows. Many other groups call such shows "industrials." When we perform for a high-tech firm, the Oregon Medical Association, or a law firm, I'm almost always included because I understood how to interact with them. If a lawyer mentions a case or an area of law, there is a good chance I've heard of it or encountered the concepts.

My experience in the defense industry, and as a technical writer who authors books on Microsoft Excel, means that I can speak directly to suggestions dealing with software, database management, accounting, electronics, and, in some cases, engineering. Many other players in our group can do the same for fields including theatre (no surprise there), advertising, software development, counseling, insurance, systems science, and visual arts. That variety makes for very strong group because it allows us to work off of each other in many different ways and learn from each other.

Translating Among Dialects

Performing with many of the same people for more than 15 years has allowed my improv group to develop a deep connections. Our shared experiences allow us to communicate quickly by referring to something that happened, even if that's not in the recent past. It can be difficult for new members of the group to pick up on these cues immediately, but we try to be welcoming, answer any questions, and provide context when we realize that something we said might not be immediately understood.

Few things are more frustrating than a conversation where the participants do not share a set of common assumptions. This type of situation can occur when you travel. Words have different meanings depending on the location or context. I stumbled across a wonderful example in Frank Jacobs' Strange Maps blog on The Big Think. On August 18, 2008, Jacobs published a map of the regional variances for referring to soft drink products such as Coca-Cola. In some parts of the United States, you call it cola, in others soda, and in still others pop. My lawyer friend, Kasey Christie, informed me that in a large part of the American South, including his native Texas, the term "Coke" is actually the generic term for any sort of soda pop. I'm sure the Coca-Cola Company loves that their product's branding has penetrated so far into Southern society (the company is based in Atlanta), but generic usage of the term in the media could put their trademark in jeopardy.

You can also find different dialects and means of communication within companies. One of the most common differences is between non-technical managers and engineers. Scott Adams, who writes the *Dilbert* comic strip, does a great job of lampooning these relationships. Managers, or marketers for that matter, know what they want and are not afraid to ask the engineers to violate the laws of physics to make it happen. You also find frequent disconnects between technical support representatives and customers. Customers often think they know everything there is to know about a program after using it for a short period and use specialized vocabulary to describe what they think is going wrong when they call for support. The problem is that many times they don't understand the words they're using, especially not in an engineering context, so they end up adding more confusion to the process.

You'll also find similar problems on design teams, even among team members who are trained in the same discipline. Different schools and instructors describe techniques and phenomena differently, so it can be difficult to communicate effectively when you think you have a shared meaning because you use similar terms in the expected context.

The best way to clear up any potential misunderstanding is to paraphrase what you think has been communicated and, if possible, draw it out on a whiteboard or in a document that you e-mail to your colleague. You take a risk by committing yourself in writing, but doing so facilitates communication and will get you closer to your ultimate goal, which is a successful design. You do need to be ready for feedback, just in case there is a disconnect between you and your colleague, but it is far better to identify confusion or disagreement at the beginning of an interaction than after you've put in significant time working on what turns out to be incorrect assumptions.

4

Listening, Processing, and Reacting

Everything that happens in an improv scene is an offer, something that adds detail to a scene and invites you to expand on it. Whether you are getting a suggestion from an audience member, reacting to another player, or thinking about what was said in the instant before you react, what you do should build upon what has come before. This consideration takes us back to the principle of "Yes, and." Everything you do should be consistent with what has come before, even if you are offering something new. Conflicting information doesn't necessarily mean you're saying "no." Instead, what you say could acknowledge what has gone before as being true, while offering information that creates a conflict within the scene.

In this chapter, I'll talk about the three elements of accepting and working with information: listening, processing, and reacting. Listening seems easy, but it's a lot harder than it seems. Many people think they're good listeners, but in fact what they're doing is waiting for the occurrence of keywords that let them insert content they've prepared a point to interject. Processing is how you relate what you've heard to what you already know. In an improv context, that could mean adding information to a scene, understanding how what you've heard fits into the plot as it's developed, or formulating a response. Reacting takes the final step and embodies some sort of an extension from what has gone before. In an improv sense, reacting means you acknowledge and extend what has been said or done. Your reaction can be verbal, physical, emotional, or any combination of the three.

Listening

At its most basic level, listening means accepting input from an audible source. It sounds simple, but surprisingly few people listen well, in large part because they have an agenda other than gaining information.

In 1996, John Kline wrote a book entitled *Listening Effectively* for Air University Press. Air University is the United States Air Force's professional development organization. The school makes its unclassified study materials available for free on the school's website since it is funded by taxpayer dollars. In this book, Kline discussed the 6 fallacies of listening, named 5 bad habits that prevent individuals from listening effectively, and delved into the listening process. He also described several different types of listening: informative listening, relationship listening, appreciative listening, critical listening, and discriminative listening.

Informative listening, or listening to understand, is what most people mean when they discuss listening. When you engage in informative listening, you want to take in data that helps you make decisions. In an improv context, you need to engage in informative listening throughout the scene. Because you're creating everything on the spot, you must pay very close attention so you can create a performance that is consistent with what is gone before. Names, places, and events are all things that your fellow players might mention during the scene. There are few things more embarrassing during an improv game than calling someone by the wrong name.

In business, you also engage in informative listening. One recent trend in business presentations is to limit the number of slides you can use during a presentation. Some companies insist that you only have three slides and your presentation may last for no more than seven minutes, while others give you one slide and five minutes. You also might be familiar with the Ignite series of presentations that go on around the world. In an Ignite presentation you have 20 slides, each of which is displayed for 15 seconds, which means you have 5 minutes to speak. At the end of your five minutes, someone else walks on stage, grabs the microphone, and starts their talk. When I worked in Washington, DC, I had a boss who was fond of saying "Don't tell me what I already know. I only want new information." I pass this advice along to you so that you can save your executives' and colleagues' time.

You can use the "Tell Me More" exercise to explore subjects in conversation. Have someone start talking about a subject and, if they use a term of art or a phrase you want to delve into, say "tell me more about that" and let them provide more detail.

Relationship listening is all about building rapport with people. During relationship listening, you're not really listening for information, although you should be alert in case anything important is revealed. Instead, your goal should be to improve the relationship between you and the speaker. Relationship listening gets a bad rap among guys, mainly because we're not very good at it–at least that's the stereotype. Beer companies and their ad agencies have created countless commercials in which a guy is able to sneak out of the house by giving his wife or girlfriend a few minutes of listening time before running down to a bar to do what he really wants to do, which is hang with his guy friends.

Relationship listening does occur during improv scenes, especially if you're performing a long form show that could up to an hour. When you're doing long form improv you have two

31

goals: to entertain your audience and to fill the time. As long as there is a sense of progression, which could mean furthering the action or deepening a relationship, it's okay to have relationship listening during an improv scene. In short form, scenes typically last no more than 4 or 5 minutes. Relationship listening can occur but it needs to happen at a much faster clip. You're trying to communicate that you are performing relationship listening and then move on with the action of the scene.

The next type of listening is *appreciative listening*. As the name implies, appreciative listening occurs when you appreciate something such as music, a play, or a speaker. The late Steve Jobs was famous for setting up what was called a "reality distortion field." Whenever he introduced an Apple product, he communicated his excitement about a product in such a way that people in the audience were completely swept up by their enthusiasm.

When you create an improv scene, your goal is to convince the audience that they want to engage in appreciative listening. Very few improv scenes are without flaws. It's just part of the nature of creating something on the fly. I remember watching a videotape of a musical comedy performed by the Los Angeles ComedySportz group. It was a 45-minute musical murder mystery. The first time through, everything was wonderful. All the plot points were there, there didn't seem to be any contradictions in the story, and so on. However, the second time I watched the video, I noticed quite a few flaws. Watching the performance a second time did not reduce my enjoyment, but it did point out how easy it was for me to overlook the flaws the first time through.

As a fellow performer and as a business person, appreciative listening can be dangerous. It's very easy for your fellow performers to get caught up during scene, but if you're not thinking critically about what you're hearing, your ability to contribute will be limited. Just as you shouldn't laugh at your own jokes, neither should you enjoy what your fellow performers are doing so much that you become distracted. By the same token, when you're listening to a business presentation, always keep your critical faculties alert. Of course you'll think a product is cool or you'll like the presenter or the message. You should always maintain a critical outlook that will let you make decisions based on something other than the emotion of the moment.

That brings me to Kline's next type of listening: *critical listening*. Engaging in critical listening means that you are evaluating what is being said in terms of its truth, completeness, and usefulness. Every one of these considerations weighs heavily when evaluating what we hear. You can disregard any conclusions based on information that you deem untrue. Political commentators like to pose "what if" scenarios based on unverified media reports of an action or motivation and then go on hours-long diatribes that occasionally refer back to the original hypothetical statement occasionally. Using this tactic leads the audience to become involved in the discussion of the consequences. They gradually forget that the foundational statement may or may not be true. For anyone who tunes in after a disclaimer about the statement's accuracy, they might assume the statement is true because they have not been informed otherwise.

Kline's final type of listening is *discriminative listening*. In this case, "discriminative" means to listen with the goal of discovering meaning through sensitivity to body language, tone, pace, and other aspects of speech apart from the words used. Discriminative listening is challenging for individuals who have a hard time recognizing body language. The stereotypical computer nerd is notoriously insensitive to body language and nuance, so much so that sarcasm and irony are lost on them. Body language and vocal nuance vary so much from region to region, it's a wonder we can understand anything but the most basic statements in our native language.

Listening in an Improv Scene

Listening in an improv scene takes on a very strange set of characteristics. Some writers would tell you to turn off your critical listening skills entirely. After all, it's very hard to say "Yes, and" to whatever comes along if you're listening critically and making judgments about what you hear.

I disagree.

Obviously, you will be doing a lot of informative listening. You need to know what is going on in the scene, contribute to it, and recognize when your offering has been used, or if your scene partner has decided to go in a separate direction. Let's say you intend for the scene to take place on a submarine. You need to make it very clear when you initiate the scene where you are. It can be a lot of fun, and in fact wonderfully fun, if you slide down a periscope and one of your scene partners comes in and asks when the order of French fries will be ready for Table 4. If you are the cook or another server and use the periscope to spy on your customers, you have the makings of terrific scene. On the other side of the coin, confusion about names within a scene can lead to chaos. There are few things that break down the reality of an improv scene faster than calling the same person by multiple names.

Relationship listening also plays an important role in improv scenes. Characters in a scene should know each other and have strong relationships. Establishing a strong relationship at the beginning of the scene lets you skip all the mundane "getting to know you" conversation that doesn't move the action. In many cases you are actually combining relationship listening with informative listening because you are making up the details of the relationship as you go along.

You will find that your critical listening skills are often put to the test in an improv scene. Improvisers are constantly told to turn off their inner censor and to just say what comes to mind. If you are presented with a situation and given multiple offers to choose from then, even if only on the subconscious level, you will have to choose which offer to accept and which to ignore. Most of your critical thinking will occur after the scene and, in fact, after the show. The more you can remember about what happened during scene, the offers it contained, and the choices you made, the better you will be able to analyze what you did, and why, and share that with your teammates.

As I mentioned before, comedy is highly dependent upon nuance and body language. Theater people, of which improvisers are a distinct but meaningful subset, make their living through the use of subtext, nuance, body language, and vocal inflection. It is exceptionally difficult to be a good improviser without understanding body language and nuance. What you can't get away without, however, is appreciative listening.

In many cases you need to act like you are enjoying what someone else is saying or doing, but all the while you are paying attention to the information being passed along so that you can make your own decisions. In ComedySportz, which uses the metaphor of a sports competition to frame the show, any players who aren't on the field should always be ready to jump on if another player is called for. If all the other team's players are on the field and the scene is screaming out for a waiter to pour water, a mechanic to change the oil, or a flock of wild geese, the players on the other team should be ready and willing to take on those roles.

Listening in Business

In many ways, listening in business is exactly the same as listening during an improv scene. You and your colleagues are moving toward the same goal and, even if there is a plan, not all the details are finalized. As contributors move forward on their own tasks, they will need to listen to their colleagues and give information to allow everyone to combine what they're doing into a coherent whole. That coherent whole will be defined by product plans, official documentation, and goals set by management. Everyone on a project must listen to what's going on so that they can acquire the information they need.

The roles of relationship listening, critical listening, and discriminative listening should all be clear. You need to establish and maintain good relationships with your coworkers, discover the information that is most relevant to you, and pay attention to emphasis so you can understand nuance. In a business context, appreciative listening is difficult. Normally when you think of appreciative listening, you imagine yourself listening to music. Of course, if you look at management and motivational techniques as persuasive endeavors, leadership and manage start to become performance art. The problem is that many times motivational speeches that are meant to be listened to in an appreciative mode fail miserably when listened to in a critical mode.

The motivation industry rakes in billions of dollars a year. One company, Despair.com, takes the opposite approach. Its Demotivators product line spreads the cynicism and ironic humor. I recommend its work highly, but make sure the products fit into your organization's culture.

A Useful Listening Exercise

Here's a classic exercise that will teach you how to listen more effectively. Sit down with a friend or family member and ask a question. Listen to the entire answer and then ask another question that starts with the last letter of the sentence they just finished.

This forces you to do two things: to listen to the content of the sentence and also to listen all the way to the end so you can figure out the last letter of the sentence that she gave you and then base your question from that.

As an example, let's say the dialogue goes like this:

You: *Where did you go on your last vacation?*

Her: *We went to the Bahamas and spent a lot of time on the beac<u>h</u>.*

You: *<u>H</u>ow much time per day did you spend on the beach?*

Her: *About three hour<u>s</u>.*

You: *<u>S</u>o I guess you went through a lot of sunscreen.*

Her: *We di<u>d</u>.*

You: *<u>D</u>o you plan to go back?*

Her: *Yes we're hoping to go back next yea<u>r</u>.*

> *You: Repeat vacations are fun. It's always interesting to*
> *see how the place stands up on the second visit.*

This exercise reinforces a basic component of listening: ensuring that the speaker has finished their thought. This turn-taking exercise seems to fly in the face of most modern conversation. When you get a group of friends together, such as in a bar for drinks or over dinner, you can usually expect a freely flowing conversation in which individuals take turns as required and pay attention to others when it's obviously their turn to speak.

The problem comes when someone finishes someone else's sentence and then doesn't return the floor to the person who was originally speaking. It is worse when someone interjects and drives a conversation in a direction that they want to go, regardless of the desires of the rest of the group.

Processing

After you've listened to your colleagues, whether in an improv scene or in a business situation, you can process the information. Humans process information remarkably quickly, and we are tempted to respond immediately. Many situations, including those during an improv scene, demand a quick response, but they do not demand an *immediate* response. In improv, your first reaction is almost always the right one. When the scene is flowing well, and you have a good connection with your scene partners, you'll just know what to say next. You can choose to pause for effect or, if you can't think of an immediate response that either fits within the context of the scene or within the parameters of the show, it's perfectly fine to react nonverbally. Your reaction might be to turn away and have an emotional moment, which is just as valid and provides as much information as a verbal response.

What's happening behind the scenes when you process information—meaning, what's going on your head? A lot of it has to do with what you remember from the scene, your time with the group, and your life experiences.

Institutional Memory

It might seem odd to speak of an improvisational comedy group as having an institutional memory, but most of them do. As with any other group of individuals, institutional memory comes from having long-term members of the group who are able and willing to pass the lessons they've learned to newer members.

In the fall of 2010, I played in a ComedySportz show at the state gathering for the Harley-Davidson Owners Group, or H.O.G. Before the show, several of us pulled out our mobile phones and did some research on Harley-Davidson as a company and motorcycle culture. We found a list of motorcycle terms we could use and, it must be said, quite a few that we couldn't.

Road shows, like the one we played for the H.O.G., can provide some logistical challenges. To add some certainty to the process, we bring our own sound system. You never know what will be present at the venue. When you bring your own gear, you also have to set up and tear down. Over the years, you develop a feel for the rooms that you work in and can determine whether you need two speakers or four, whether the players need wireless microphones, or whether they can just work with their natural voices. There's also the physical task of setting up the sound system. With an amplifier, CD player, and wireless microphones for the players, you have a lot of inputs going into your board. You need to manage their volumes so that everyone can be heard and everyone's levels are about the same.

Many new players are brought up and given the opportunity to perform as the sound player. At our home shows, that means the new players can watch the show and participate. Some of the sound player's duties are to play music, make announcements, and provide sound effects for the scenes. Pitching in this way helps newer players gain a feel for the show by watching several of them and participating from the sound booth.

Being Part of a Larger Organization

One of the advantages of being a ComedySportz player is that we are truly a worldwide organization. At present, we have teams in 20 U.S. cities, plus 2 in Europe. Not only do we share ideas within teams, but representatives from each city also gather at our league tournament every year. At tournaments, players from different cities lead workshops in all areas of improvisational comedy. In past years, there have been workshops on character development, accents (especially those of the British Isles), Shakespeare, singing, and storytelling. Each of these workshops ranges in duration from an hour to 4 hours and helps attendees develop a specific set of skills. In most cases, the workshop leader can combine the exercises with ComedySportz games so the skills will have immediate application. After they return to their home cities, players can share what they learned with their colleagues.

Another benefit of a tournament is that you can communicate with players from other cities and find out which games they play. This will help you discover best practices for those games. We've been lucky in Portland because we've had players from several other cities join us when they moved here. We have players from Dallas, Houston, and San Jose on our current roster. Every city plays games a little differently, so when you gather together at tournament you can discover and explore the differences in your workshops and in tournament shows. It isn't until someone moves from one city to another, however, that you can truly gain significant insights into how other cities run their shows and play their games. Some games are extremely popular with some cities but are rarely played in others. Also, even if the games are the same, there can be conventions that differ from city to city. Any time visiting players come to Portland, we make sure they understand how we're going to play each game. Minor differences can trip you up unless you discuss them beforehand.

There are very few professional improvisational comedians in the world. In Portland, we do have a number of members of the group who make most if not all their living from performance. The rest of us have other jobs. At present we have two technical writers, numerous software developers, a speech pathologist, a counselor working toward her Ph.D., a recruiter, an animal control officer, two network architects, a camera store manager, two individuals who give walking tours of Portland, and a puppeteer. When you combine all those different skills and abilities with our varying backgrounds, there is a wide range of experiences and knowledge that, with time, leads to a diverse specialties within the group. It's not very often that we get a suggestion that one of the players in the show hasn't heard of. We always have a wider age range than most groups. Most of our 40 active players are in their late 20s to early 40s, but we have a very talented college student (who started in our Middle School League) who joins us when he's in town and a couple of players who are in their early 60s.

War Stories

Almost everyone in ComedySportz looks forward to the annual tournament, where the learning experience intensifies. A number of us keep in touch throughout the year on the organization's web forums. We have a range of discussion areas, ranging from topics specific to ComedySportz, to issues specific to a given city or team.

One of the best ways to pass on important information is to relate what happened on a trip, in a game, or during warm-ups. The more you know about the variety of situations you can face and how to handle them, the better off you are. Stephen Denning emphasizes the value of these stories in *A Leader's Guide to Storytelling*:

> Listening to these stories isn't merely entertainment: it leads to the acquisition of vicarious experience by those participating. The limitation of sharing stories in an informal setting is that those who aren't present to learn. This limitation was overcome by the Xerox Corporation in its Eureka program, in which photocopy technicians were given two-way radios so they could be constantly in contact and share experiences; the most useful of the stories were vetted and made available on the web to the entire workforce of 25,000 technicians.

In addition to our online forums, ComedySportz maintains an internal wiki of games and warm-ups. A *wiki* is a shared database of information that can be edited by any member of the group. Wikipedia is the most prominent example of a public wiki.

The Portland team also has occasional workshops in which

individual players get 10–15 minutes to share knowledge on a topic we're comfortable with. Some companies have brown-bag lunches based on a similar theme. One project I haven't started yet, but hope to soon, is something I borrowed from a former boss at The MITRE Corporation. He sent out a survey asking what languages people spoke, what skills they had, and so on. A spreadsheet or database that contains this information can be extremely valuable when a situation arises and you need someone who can read Guajarati or can recommend a business hotel in the South Kensington area of London.

In a conference keynote address, I suggested that rural telephone companies and co-operatives have their technicians call in to a central voice mail number and record the details of a repair job. The company could then transcribe the recording using Dragon Naturally Speaking or other software and put the results in a searchable text database.

Reacting

Human reactions can often be a mystery. Most of the time, you go through your day without anything surprises, only to find that one little thing, something that wouldn't normally bother you, sets you off. You might be a frequent plane traveler who can sit through most noise without being bothered. Then, for no discernable reason, on a cross-country flight after a particularly long day, you don't care about the baby crying two rows behind you but find that the breath whistling through your neighbor's nose is intensely annoying.

Popular literature analyzing why we react the way they do has exploded over the last few years. One of the most useful is the book *Thinking, Fast and Slow* by Nobel Prize winner Daniel Kahneman. Kahneman breaks down thinking into two broad categories: System 1 and System 2. System 1 is the automatic reaction we have to circumstances. For example, someone could ask you for the name of a flower and you would say *rose*. System 1 is the automatic reaction that comes to mind without any sort of mediation. System 2, on the other hand, allows for reflective thinking, consideration, and doubt. System 1 is for thinking fast, while System 2 is for thinking slow.

Kahneman identifies how individuals can be primed to think of something. In an improv context, moderators often ask for suggestions regarding a subject. They might ask for a flower, a celebrity, or an outdoor activity. If an audience just watched a scene relating to one of the mentioned topics, the first thing that comes to mind will often be something referenced in that scene. Retailers use this technique to prepare you to spend money when you walk into the store and to convince you to make impulse buys on your way to the checkout counter.

As an improviser, it can be very tempting to let yourself fall back on a series of automatic reactions. If you play with a group for a long time, you'll find that audiences offer the same suggestions fairly frequently. Obviously, you can alter what you request to reduce this repetition, but eventually audiences will repeat themselves. It's amazing how narrowly popular attention can be focused.

If you want to avoid burnout, you need to introduce variety into your performances. That can mean getting suggestions and categories you don't normally ask for, having individuals who don't normally play together start a scene to generate some unique interaction, or enter a scene as a character of a type you wouldn't normally play. I tend to play fairly technical, high-status characters. I'm a nerd by inclination, so it's most natural for me to take on that sort of character. If I want to change things up, I might come in as a female character or perhaps a high school dropout.

I cringe whenever I hear an improviser say, "Whenever someone does this, I always do that." If you have multiple people doing that, you always get the same result. In ComedySportz, we have two games that rely on this gimmick: Mr. So-and-So and Pavlovian Response. In Mr. So-and-So, every time a player comes on stage, another player endows him with a particular characteristic. For example, a player could walk on stage and be greeted with, "Hello Mr. Yawns When He Talks." When the player honors that endowment, he will yawn whenever he opens his mouth to speak.

Even though I say you shouldn't repeat gags as you go along, I know that players with any significant experience will have characters and bits they can go back to when needed. They're fine in small doses, but don't depend on them.

In the game of Pavlovian Response, every player is given a trigger and an action that occurs whenever the trigger is noticed. A player might bark like a dog whenever someone turns away from her. You can have a lot of fun chaining these reactions together. Perhaps, upon hearing the word the, a player could respond by leaving the stage. Another player could be assigned to clap her hands twice whenever someone leaves the stage. If you want to get crazy, you can endow the light operator to turn the lights on or off whenever someone claps their hands twice.

In offstage life, not every interaction has to be unique. Companies have policies and procedures in place for very good reasons: legal compliance, standards compliance, and maintaining audit trails. For example, if you're in a customer-facing position, you need to have a series of procedures you work through to be sure you weed out the simplest and easiest-to-fix problems. (You're attempting to save your time at the expense of your customer's time, but that's another story.)

One of the best interactions I've had with the company happened very recently. My house has a watering system from Rain Bird. After a power outage, the system turned on, and the only way to get it to turn off was to unplug the system's control board. After working through the manual, neither my wife nor I could get the system to reset correctly. I called the company's toll-free help line and, after a couple of questions to verify my information, the technician simply asked me to describe what was going on. Using his expertise with the systems, he was able to guide me to a solution very quickly. This interaction represented the best combination of procedure and allowing for open-ended input that I've encountered in quite some time.

In the end, your best bet as an improviser is to embrace the reality of the scene as you and your fellow performers have created it, and allow yourself to go in new directions. In business, you need to be ready to face the unexpected, but you should rely on existing procedures that help ensure smooth operations within your company.

5

The Games within the Games

It might seem odd to bring up a formal game theory in a book on improvisation and how it applies to business. In fact, we can learn a lot from the four basic games: Chicken, Battle of the Sexes, Stag Hunt, and the Prisoner's Dilemma. Each of these games has a direct application to both business relationships and improvisational comedy performances. In this chapter, I will describe the four basic games, show how they apply to both business and improv situations, and offer tips on how to manage the situation if you find yourself playing one of the games. I'll spend most of my time on the Prisoner's Dilemma, so I'll deal with it last.

The Four Basic Games

Each of the games I'll cover in this chapter uses a 2 x 2 matrix for payoffs. The games are competitive – your goal is to accumulate the highest possible score. You are also playing blind, so you have no idea what the other player's choice will be and no way to communicate, except through your choices within the game. That means playing the game once is very different from playing it several times, or not at all. I'll start with the game that's easiest to visualize: Chicken.

Chicken

If you've watched any movies from the 1950s about disaffected youth, you are surely familiar with the game of Chicken. In the game of Chicken, two cars face each other. At a signal, they drive toward each other at high speed. The first driver to swerve loses – that person is the chicken. As with all of our 2 x 2 games, there are four ways this game can play out.

The payoffs appear in the following table.

	Swerve	Straight
Swerve	0, 0	-1, 1
Straight	1, -1	-10, -10

The first outcome is if both drivers swerve, which results in payoffs of zero. Both drivers swerve, so that means that neither of them won. But, because the outcome was equal, neither of them lost, either. The next two outcomes occur when one driver swerves and the other stays straight. In that case, we do have a clear winner and a clear loser, which is reflected in the payoffs of plus one for the winner and minus one for the loser. In the fourth case, disaster strikes. In that case, neither driver swerves and there is a high-speed, head-on collision.

This game can be used to analyze both improv and business. When you create an improv scene, someone has to give up control. Even if it's only for a moment, players must accept what other players say and do so everyone can continue to build a consistent reality without interrupting the audience's enjoyment. The best outcome in a game of Chicken when you're performing an improv scene is to have one player swerve and one player continue straight on. That means one player made a solid decision and all the other player has to do is follow along and build on what is been established. If both players swerve, that means no one is taking the reins and attempting to drive the scene forward.

I should also note that in an improv scene and in business you play multiple games of Chicken. Every time someone makes a decision during an improv scene, the other players have to decide whether to accept it or move on to something else. Yes, there are times when you have to set aside something that has been said because it isn't germane to what's been going on, but usually whatever has been said should be accepted and incorporated.

In business, one of the most common ways to play Chicken is what's called *Schedule Chicken*. In Schedule Chicken, managers face off against each other in a meeting room and none of them is willing to admit that they will not meet their deadline. Because they agreed to a schedule at the start of the project, whoever blinks will be blamed for causing the project to slip if they have to ask for more time.

Unrealistic schedules are deadly. In her *Harvard Business Review* article "How to Kill Creativity", Teresa M. Amibile notes:

> Organizations routinely kill creativity with fake deadlines or impossibly tight ones. The former create distrust and the latter cause burnout.

In business, it can be tough to admit that you will not meet schedule deadlines. If the other managers or workers on a team say that they can make their deadlines with no problem, it means that you are the one causing the slip. Of course, it might be complete fiction that the other teams could have been ready in time, but if you're the first one to admit that you won't make it, you're the one who gets the blame.

How you solve the game of Schedule Chicken depends on your corporate culture. Companies that refuse to ship until the product is ready reduce the possibility of Schedule Chicken, especially if they don't set final deadlines until the project is well underway. For multiyear efforts, final deadlines and announcements should be kept out of the press as long as possible. Companies that use agile development and roll out small updates frequently avoid Schedule Chicken by shipping when the update is ready, and not announcing times until the next increment is ready to go.

Battle of the Sexes

The *Battle of the Sexes* game sets up a situation in which neither player can get their preferred outcome, but the worst possible outcome is disagreeing. Let's say you and your partner are invited to a party, and the host has asked you to bring beer or wine, but not both. Now also assume that you can't get in contact with your partner. It's the lack of coordination that makes these 2 x 2 games interesting and aggravating.

	Beer	Wine
Beer	3, 2	0, 0
Wine	0, 0	2, 3

For the sake of argument, let's assume that you are a beer drinker and your partner prefers wine. For you, the best possible outcome is if both you and your partner decide to bring beer. The second-best outcome is if both of you decide to bring wine, and tied for the worst are when you and your partner bring different beverages. The problem is that you have no way to decide whether to bring beer or wine. If you base your decision on your partner's preferences, you will bring wine. On the other hand, if you think that your partner will go along with your choice, you will bring beer. There's no way to place one of those two options over the other. What's worse is that your partner has exactly the same problem.

In terms of improv, you'll find the Battle of the Sexes come into play when communication falters before a scene or game. Every improv group plays games differently, even when they're based on the same pattern. If you go over to one side of the stage to pick up a costume piece before conferring with your playing partners, whoever starts might not have the same idea about how to play the game as everyone else. A train wreck will ensue if your scene partners play one game, and you're playing another. It's easy enough to fix once everything gets underway either you or your playing partners can adapt, but there might be an awkward moment or two at the start. At that point, you just hope the audience either doesn't notice or forgives you.

In business, you'll find that the Battle of the Sexes game is played out during sales calls and engineering meetings. Everyone has a preferred solution for implementing a change or creating a product. Any time there are multiple pathways to creating a product or finishing a project, you should be in close communication to ensure that the solution you're pursuing doesn't contradict what someone else is doing.

Stag Hunt

The Stag Hunt game is also called the Assurance Game or the Coordination Game. The basic idea behind the Stag Hunt is that the players can increase their payoff by cooperating. Following one traditional way to state the game's conditions, I'll define cooperation as a situation in which two individuals can increase their immediate payoffs by working together.

In its traditional form, the Stag Hunt frames the game around two hunters. The hunters can either choose to hunt for a stag, which has a very high payoff, or a hare, which has a small payoff. Every time you hunt for a hare you will catch one and get a small payoff. On the other hand, if you hunt for a stag and the other hunter goes after a hare, you will get nothing, and the other hunter will get the hare. You get a stag only if both of you decide to go after it. That's why this game is also called the Coordination Game: You must coordinate your efforts to get the highest possible return.

The following matrix displays the payoffs for the Stag Hunt.

	Stag	Hare
Stag	3, 3	0, 1
Hare	1, 0	1, 1

As with most of the other classic 2 x 2 games, we assume that the hunters can't communicate. At least, not so that they can coordinate their efforts before they choose which strategy to follow. What they can see, however, are the payoffs after they play a round of the game. This situation leads to some very interesting outcomes, especially when you consider it across species.

The authors of a paper titled "Responses to the Assurance Game in Monkeys, Apes, and Humans," using equivalent procedures, tested whether capuchin monkeys, chimpanzees, or humans would perform better at the Assurance Game. The researchers chose these primates because they all show tendencies toward cooperation in their natural environment. Significantly, the humans were not allowed to talk during the testing.

As you might expect, the humans performed better than either the chimpanzees or the capuchin monkeys, but the difference was not as great as one might expect. The researchers found that the humans who discovered the hare-hare approach thought that they had beaten the game, and always received a reliable payoff. Game theorists call this approach the *risk dominant strategy*. Once the players achieve a reliable outcome, they tend not to move away from it and explore alternate possibilities.

The paper's authors summarized their results this way:

> Finally, despite being the species for which the highest frequency of pairs achieved the payoff dominant outcome, even among humans fewer than 20% in pairs did so (this increases to 27% when borderline pairs are included). An additional 38% of pairs achieved the risk dominant outcome (hare-hare), and 12% matched their partner. It is worth reiterating that despite success of humans compared with the other primates, a nontrivial proportion of pairs failed to achieve the payoff-dominant outcome. This underscores the difficulty of finding outcomes when the typical human procedures (instructions, payoff matrices, pretest for understanding) are absent, common handicaps for nonhuman species.

Obtaining the highest possible payoff from any venture, whether it is in improv or in business, means taking risks. Even in this artificial situation, where communication was limited, some humans managed to find the payoff-dominant outcome for the Stag Hunt experiment. But many of them did not. As the authors of the study note, this is most likely a case of humans being risk averse. In an improv context, being risk averse might mean always asking for the same type of suggestions or doing the same type of scene, regardless of which suggestion you get. Some so-called improv groups even get a single suggestion from the audience, use it once by stating it during their scene, and then do the rest of the scene according to a script. It's a cheat, one that takes a lot of the fun out of performing unless you change the script every night. It does reduce the risk of having something go terribly wrong and not entertaining your audience. Over time, however, taking larger risks will yield greater rewards as long as you have competent performers.

Starting a new business, creating a new product, or offering a new service is risky. All of your effort could be for naught if you've misjudged your market, your customers, or the desirability of your product. It is possible to adjust, perhaps by reducing the price of your product or by adding new services. In the end there is always the risk that you will not see sufficient return on your investment.

One of the ways that ComedySportz reduces risk is by adhering to a show structure. We developed our current format over 25 years and by performing many thousands of shows. We have found that our pace, internal structure, and audience involvement work consistently and well. We feel comfortable taking risks because we trust our fellow performers and we know that even if one game doesn't succeed, there will be more for the audience to enjoy. Just as the Stag Hunt game is meant to build cooperation and find a payoff-dominant outcome, the more we work together and find ways to have fun on stage, the more successful we are as a group and as individual performers.

Prisoner's Dilemma

The *Prisoner's Dilemma* is perhaps the classic 2 x 2 game. The scenario is simple enough to explain, but it seems impossible to find a way out of the dilemma. Here's the situation: You and a fellow criminal have been apprehended, and the police want at least one of you to give evidence against the other guy. They say if neither of you talks, they have enough evidence to put each of you in jail for a relatively short time. On the other hand, if you give up the other guy and he refuses to talk, he will be convicted and sentenced to a long term, and you will go free. Of course, if you don't talk and he does, the same thing happens to you. If you both talk, you will each get a sentence that's worse than you would get if you were the only one to defect, but not as bad as when you didn't confess and your partner in crime did.

You can summarize the Prisoner's Dilemma payoffs using the following 2 x 2 grid.

	Cooperate	Defect
Cooperate	-1, -1	-5, 0
Defect	0, -5	-3, -3

The question is this: What is the best way to play this game? Obviously, it's in your best interest to cooperate. If you both cooperate (that is, you cooperate with each other and don't talk), you will get a sentence of only one year and minimize the negative payoff. The problem is that if the other individual knows that you are going to cooperate, he has no incentive to play along. He should defect (turn you in and get away with no jail time at all). To avoid the possibility of a longer jail term, you should also turn in the other person, giving him a medium sentence and ensuring that you don't get the longest possible prison term.

So, the strategy for playing the Prisoner's Dilemma just once is to defect. You don't get the best possible payoff, but you do prevent yourself from getting the worst possible outcome. The same considerations work for improv and business. If you never plan on performing or working with someone again, what they think of you and what they might do to you in the future is irrelevant. You could choose to defect by breaking a promise or paying an invoice late and move on with your life knowing that the other individual or business won't be able to exact revenge. But what if you play game multiple times? That's what's called an Iterated Prisoner's Dilemma.

Improv groups and businesses are meant to be long-lived entities. The group I'm with, ComedySportz Portland, has been around since 1993 – as of this writing, that means we've been around for 20 years. I like to joke that means we have lasted 40 times longer than the average improv group. There are plenty of improv groups that have been around for a long time, but many more that implode in very short order.

Why do some groups stay together and others break apart? One thing that can make it happen is taking advantage of the other individuals in your group, whether by not making good on your promises or by not cooperating during scenes. You can be uncooperative by making personal comments at another player's expense, such as about their weight, height, or the choices that they made; denying other players' choices during a scene or game; or showing up late (or not at all) to a rehearsal or performance. Taking advantage of the goodwill of your fellow players is shortsighted. Forming a successful group is difficult, so you should do your best to ensure the group you're with carries on, or at least that you don't burn any bridges if you do decide to leave.

As Robert Axelrod noted in his book, *The Evolution of Cooperation*, and Scott Stevens explained in his *Games People Play* course for The Great Courses, the more likely it is for the game to continue, the more incentive you have to continue cooperating throughout the game. The same consideration applies to business relationships. Con artists can get money out of their victims and disappear knowing that, if their luck holds, they will never have to encounter that individual again. For business professionals, you have to take the opposite approach. Even though many of us change jobs and industries, it's very likely that we will encounter the same faces repeatedly during our career. We should cultivate the best relationships we can. In game theoretic terms, that means we should cooperate whenever possible.

Axelrod held a tournament among computer programs playing the Prisoner's Dilemma. Every program played every other program, a second copy of itself, and a program Axelrod created that randomly chose whether to cooperate or defect. In that first tournament, which had 14 entrants, a program by Anatol Rapoport named *Tit for Tat* won. The strategy behind Tit for Tat is simple: Start out by cooperating, but if the other player defects, defect on the next turn as punishment. If the other player doesn't defect again on the next turn, switch back to cooperating.

So why would this program win? As Stevens points out in his course, the best the program can hope to do is to tie. It never tries to take advantage of the other player, so it will never get a higher payoff in any round than the other program. What's important to understand is that Tit for Tat minimized its losses.

It punished other programs for defecting, but it only did so once if there was just a single defection. This strategy of minimizing its own losses while minimizing the other programs' gain due to bad behavior made Tit for Tat the best program of the bunch.

Tit for Tat won because it elicited cooperation. Axelrod noted that the program is nice, provokable, forgiving, and straightforward. Among humans playing the game, or for computer programs with a memory of past turns, playing Tit for Tat lets other players accurately predict the consequences of their actions.

In the first Prisoner's Dilemma tournament, the top eight programs were all nice, which meant that they were never the first to defect. The participants included a program called JOSS, which was the same as Tit for Tat but threw in the occasional defection at random. The program was meant to take advantage of the occasionally high payoff from an unchallenged defection while retaining the benefits of cooperation. Unfortunately, this strategy resulted in low scores because its actions weren't predictable. It created a series of moves versus Tit for Tat, and variations of Tit for Tat, in which each program defected on alternate turns and led to dismally low scores.

In Axelrod's analysis, he noted that there were three strategies not included in the tournament that, if submitted, would have won. He ran a second tournament with these results made available to potential entrants. He also randomized the number of rounds each pair of strategies competed against each other to invalidate "late round" tactics. The new competition attracted 62 entries. Tit for Tat won again. From the results, it's easy to see that there is a penalty for being the first to defect. Axelrod wrote:

> What seems to have happened is an interesting
> interaction between people who drew one lesson
> and people who drew another from the first round.
> Lesson One was: "Be nice and forgiving." Lesson
> Two was more exploitative: "If others are going to
> be nice and forgiving, it pays to try to take
> advantage of them." The people who drew Lesson
> One suffered in the second round from those who
> drew Lesson Two….The reason is that in trying to
> exploit other rules, they often eventually got
> punished enough to make the whole game less
> rewarding for both players than pure mutual
> cooperation would have been.

Lessons Learned

Axelrod's analysis gives us a number of results that we can use
both in the realm of improv and in the realm of business. He
enumerated the five principles in *The Evolution of
Cooperation*:

- Enlarge the shadow of the future

- Change the payoffs

- Teach people to care about each other

- Teach reciprocity

- Improve negotiation abilities

Enlarging the shadow of the future means taking a long view
of your interactions. When you form an improvisational
comedy group, you should plan to have many performances

over a number of months or years. This ongoing interaction, like any other relationship, requires nurturing and mutual trust. Just like saving for retirement, the more you set aside in terms of money or trust at the start, the higher your return. As the years go by, the interest accumulates. The same principle holds for business interactions. Americans on the West Coast tend to change jobs more often than folks on the East Coast, but many of us stay within the same industry and interact with our colleagues from previous jobs frequently. Within a company, you'll find that fostering a spirit of cooperation will help you generate better results.

The next question is how to reward different behaviors. In the classic Prisoner's Dilemma payoff matrix, the only logical choice is to defect. Doing so limits the damage that would be caused by trusting another individual whose is likely to defect. In business, anyone who sees their business as a series of one-time interactions will not be all that keen on building trusting relationships with their business partners. In the entertainment industry, it said that you haven't really sold someone until you've done business with them twice. If they're not willing to rehire you, it means that they don't trust you based on their experience with you.

Teaching people to care about each other can be tricky, particularly if you have individuals who are not prone to trusting. Sociopaths, who don't empathize with other individuals at all, are a particular problem. I'm not a psychologist, so I can't tell you how to deal with them, but there are a number of online resources that you can use. For individuals who do have feelings toward others, use teambuilding exercise rewards and the warm afterglow of successful shows or projects will develop a sense of camaraderie.

In the improv world, where members of local groups are reasonably equal, you won't have much trouble with these relationships. Sometimes members of the group will disagree intensely, but if everything is in place and the relationship is solid, it's likely that you will get through the difficulties. In a business in which promotions, internal awards, and raises are at issue, the stakes are higher. Managers need to balance everyone's wants, needs, and desires as they manage their projects.

Rewarding success ensures people are satisfied. The nature of those rewards will vary based on your business and the resources available to you, but rewards and recognition, even if only at the personal level, go a long way toward making those relationships more solid.

Axelrod also recommends teaching reciprocity. A willingness to respond to offers of cooperation allows teams to progress further than a loose collection of individuals. The form reciprocity takes depends upon your organization. For businesses, providing a bit of after-hours help for coworkers on a project after they have done the same for you is a perfect example. In the improv world, we can try to "set up players for the slam." Just as volleyball players run through the bump, set, spike sequence to go from defense to offense, improvisers can do their fellow players a favor by giving them straight lines, by allowing them to be the focus of the scene, and by staying off the stage when their presence is not strictly necessary. All these actions are judgment calls that get easier with experience, but managers can improve their odds, both in the performance and business worlds, by bringing on individuals who are predisposed toward reciprocity.

Finally, you should improve your negotiation skills. Negotiation is the art of the compromise, and there are very few solutions that will meet everyone's wants and desires. Some folks have to compromise, and good leaders and team members will find ways to negotiate for what they feel is necessary and compromise when it's called for.

How Cooperation Can Fail

One of Axelrod's concludes that you can maximize your payoff in a Prisoner's Dilemma tournament by following a nice strategy. That is, not defecting first. He also noted that it was possible for other strategies to beat the winner, Tit for Tat, by defecting first to get the higher payoff and then defecting every turn thereafter to ensure that the other program could never retaliate effectively. Over time, this strategy does not yield a higher payoff than the nice Tit for Tat; the strategy did not win either tournament.

But what happens if you put the nice Tit for Tat in an environment with a lot of aggressive programs? Tit for Tat will always give up the higher payoff to its opponent in the first round and get the minimum payoff in every subsequent round. Based on those rules, Tit for Tat is guaranteed to lose. If you were to put a set of strategies into a tournament, and then eliminate the bottom half of the field, Tit for Tat would always be eliminated, and the other more aggressive strategies would continue.

This type of attack is called an *invasion*. If you run a tournament and eliminate the bottom half of the field at the end of each run, you'll find certain strategies win. If you introduce even a small number of these dominant strategies into a tournament, they will eventually take over. The problem becomes even worse if you create a series of strategies that can recognize kindred spirits, enabling them to work together to maximize their payoff by cooperating.

The same behavior exists in business. In many cases when the group or company starts, everyone cooperates. Issues arise when someone who doesn't cooperate starts to achieve success. As the aggression is rewarded, others adopt the same strategy.

In time, the aggressors squeeze out the players who use a nice, cooperative strategy. It's a management headache, one that is difficult to stamp out once it gets started. Plus, as the aggressive players get promoted, the reward structure changes. Now individuals who are willing to work with the aggressive individuals are rewarded with their own promotions and expanded responsibilities.

In most cases, the company can continue under these circumstances despite the lack of trust among the players. In fact, this type of environment can fuel creativity for those people who revel in interpersonal conflict. At the same time, an organization might begin to experience problems associated with a lack of cooperation. Always looking to put one over on the other guy makes it difficult to trust anyone, especially when you're looking over your shoulder to see who will get the next promotion.

These behaviors can lead to stress, burnout, and high turnover. In a company that requires highly skilled personnel, losing a solid contributor because of a toxic work environment is costly.

In improvisational comedy groups, the same thing happens, especially at the beginning of the group's life. As people jockey for position and try to influence the group's direction, you will often find the people who started in the group either drop out, or get kicked out after they try to change the group. Well-established organizations with a solid player roster and workshops from which to bring in new players are less susceptible to this issue.

Smaller groups, such as touring companies with only four or five players, can be susceptible to issues. The trick is to select your colleagues wisely. In many cases, it's better to join another group or start a new group of your own than it is to continue on in a bad situation. Sometimes leaving a bad job is the best thing you can do.

6

Building an Effective Team

There are effective solo improvisers who can entertain an audience for an hour with nothing but a few suggestions and their own creativity. Most improv performances involve teams of three, four, or five players, but other groups are much larger and have players who perform with varying frequency based on their availability and interest. The group I'm with has fielded more than 30 different players in the last 12 months.

Companies use the interview process to determine which prospective employees to hire and evaluate who to keep on staff. Improv groups are no different. Most of the larger, well-established groups use workshops to develop newer players, and based on these players' performances, identify who to bring up to the professional level. What type of player to foster depends on the group, its goals, and its existing line-up. There are many times when you'll have quite a few players of a particular type, but with enough variation in real-life experience and playing strengths, you can maintain your group's dynamic energy.

In this chapter, I'll explain the characteristics of high-performing teams, discuss some of the traps you can fall into when efforts to maintain team unity reach dysfunctional levels, and advocate policies that help preserve team performance and creativity.

Characteristics of High-Performance Teams

Stephen Denning, formerly the director of knowledge management at the World Bank, described the characteristics of high-performance teams. Importantly, he noted that these characteristics are also the hallmarks of an effective community:

- High-performance teams shape their customers' expectations and then exceed them.

- High-performance teams rapidly adjust their performance to fit the situation.

- High-performance teams grow steadily stronger by learning one another's strengths and weaknesses, anticipating each other's next moves, and responding appropriately.

- Team members grow individually and have mutual concern for each other's personal growth, enabling members to develop interchangeable skills and greater flexibility.

- Team members make interpersonal commitments, which means the teams' goals become nobler, goals more urgent, and approach more powerful.

- High-performance teams carry out their work with a shared passion. The notion of "if one of us fails, we all fail" pervades the team.

The first element, shaping the expectations of the team's customers and then exceeding them, epitomizes team performance and how customers perceive their accomplishments. Computer manufacturer Dell is known for overestimating ship dates so their customers are ecstatic when their order arrives sooner than promised. I've ordered several computers from Dell and am well aware they overestimate shipping dates by as much as a week, but I'm still happy when my computer arrives before I expected it.

Adjusting your performance to fit the situation lies at the heart of success, whether it's on the improv stage or in business. One of the fun aspects of improv is that you never know what's going to happen next. Decisions made by your teammates change the path of your scene instantly. It's worth noting that these changes occur at the tactical level, within a game. You rarely see large-scale changes in approach during a performance. In almost every case, a team will stay with the overall framework for their show. You can always adapt an improv show for your audience by including references to their corporate culture. There's nothing an audience likes more than seeing funny parts of their lives portrayed on stage. If the scene's funny, they look like geniuses.

That's not to say that change is always good. In a *Harvard Business Review* article, Teresa M. Amibile notes that "managers undermine autonomy by continually changing goals and interfering with processes." At some point, someone has to get some work done – constantly changing workers' support structures and surroundings forces them to adapt to their new environment. This taxing thinking reduces the mental resources available for their jobs, increases stress and uncertainty, and hinders creativity.

Members of high-performance teams learn each other's strengths and weaknesses. Over time, they anticipate each other's moves and lead their teammates to success. Sports with free-flowing action and frequent passes, such as basketball, soccer, and hockey show how successful anticipation works. It's magical when one player zips a pass 50 feet on a basketball court or 50 yards on a soccer field to a teammate who just knows where to go. A solid knowledge of the game, constant practice, and communication before the fact lets you develop these skills.

Sports plays are either successful or not. It's pretty easy to tell whether a pass was on target. In improv, it's harder to tell when you're successful because you can always improv your way out of a tight spot. Each player contributes in different ways. Billy Merritt, one of the original improvisers at the Upright Citizen's Brigade in New York, identifies three types of players: pirates, robots, and ninjas.

A *pirate* is someone who just jumps on stage and makes a bold choice. Like a pirate rushing onto a ship, this player throws caution to the wind and makes something happen. When the scene is going nowhere, this type of player can be counted on to change things up. Every time you make a new choice, you have a chance for something interesting either to happen or to keep happening.

Robots are much more literal in their approach. Although the pirate can be given to flights of fancy, Merritt notes that a robot is always trying to bring a scene back to reality. That reality might be skewed by offers that have been accepted and used to shape the scene, but robots believe in consistency. Robots are terrific at tying together plots for long form improvisation. When you're putting together a 45-minute piece that is supposed to have a coherent plot, you need at least one person who can bring everything back together. That person is the robot. This is the player type I identify with most closely.

According to Merritt, *ninjas* specialize in the art of justification. In improv, justification is the art of incorporating something a scene partner just offered and making it seem like the most logical thing that could have been said or done. If you are in a scene that is set in the summer and another player hands you something, you can justify the action that they just made by pretending you have a glass of lemonade, take a drink, and act refreshed. Justification is the art of making a good decision better.

No improviser is a pure example of any of these three types, of course; they are broad but very useful stereotypes. You have probably run into this same type of grouping around your office. You have the computer nerds who know how to make the systems run but aren't always the most lively at parties, creative types who come up with fantastic ideas that have little to no basis in reality, and communicators who bridge the gap between the creatives and the techies.

Denning also observes that team members must grow individually and be concerned with each other's personal growth. This consideration is particularly important in today's rapidly changing technical environment. If you work in the technology industry, you must update your skills constantly. Business models, technologies, and programming languages change at a startling rate. The author of the book *The 5 Essential People Skills*, published by Dale Carnegie Training, advocates sending your employees to live seminars and getting them as much experience and training as possible. Setting aside the commercial motive associated with selling Dale Carnegie Training courses, the book's recommended three-step approach makes sense. The first step is to create a culture of learning, second is to have live seminars and training, and third is to create an atmosphere where ideas are valued and shared.

For improvisers, the sort of training can include going to other cities and playing with other groups, attending conferences and workshops, and sharing the ideas that you learn with your home group. In business, the opportunities for training are endless and are limited only by your organization's training budget and the amount of time you can spend away from the office.

Denning's final two points, committing to each other and the goal and working with a shared passion, require no further discussion. The more you love what you do and the more you believe in your teammates, the more effective you will be.

Group Unity and Consensus

High-performance teams require a level of cooperation and support that would seem to exclude any room for serious disagreement. That's not the case. Any group of skilled individuals will have strong opinions about tactics and strategy, so conflicts almost inevitably arise. Successful teams manage those conflicts so the team retains the ability to move forward in spite of disagreements.

How do you allow conflict while ensuring it doesn't turn into dysfunction? In a 1997 *Harvard Business Review* article, Eisenhardt, Kahwajy, and Bourgois point out that there are six tactics a company can use to manage interpersonal conflict:

- Work with more, rather than less, information and debate on the basis of facts.

- Develop multiple alternatives to enrich the level of debate.

- Share commonly agreed-upon goals.

- Inject humor into the decision process.

- Maintain a balanced power structure.

- Resolve issues without forcing consensus.

In business, you can get information about what your customers like and don't like about your products and services through market research. For businesses creating a product meant for a large audience, a lot of time and care must go into its development.

For an improvisational comedy group, the situation is much simpler. Many individuals will have lots of experience in improv and will often form their own groups or side projects with players from an existing group. Everyone can use their own interpretation of what is gone before to create something new. As astrophysicist Neil deGrasse Tyson is fond of saying, "You can have your own opinion, but you can't have your own facts." It is vitally important, both in business and improv, that you agree on the facts or given circumstances that provide the foundation for your discussion.

Improvisers develop scenes based on multiple alternatives with no object other than fun, so let's focus on business. In many cases, there is more than one way to create a product or offer a service. One of the hallmarks of the Web 2.0 generation of products and services is the agility with which you can create and modify your offerings. Even the most effective and flexible manufacturing systems require substantial time and money to switch between products. With the web, if you find something isn't working, you can change it quickly.

Sharing commonly agreed-upon goals seems easy, but can be challenging. When you work in a business, specifically for a product group, you know what you're creating. Many times, the overall design will come down from a higher level of management and you will be assigned a component of the product or program to create. You know how your part fits in with the overall product, so you can work on your element using your best judgment and with the approval of your manager.

For an improvisational comedy group, the step of setting goals for a group is difficult and ever-changing. In much the same way that Web 2.0 companies can change on the fly, improvisational comedy groups can adapt even within the middle of the scene or game. The trick is to get everyone to agree to the type of show that you want. If you offer family entertainment, do that. If you want to offer a show that focuses on political issues and aren't afraid to offend, that should be made clear. It's when you get individuals working at cross-purposes that your show can go south.

Improvisers are good with humor, which means that many of us are also able to use it as a weapon. We need to be careful so our humor doesn't detract from the seriousness of the decisions we're making. In a business context, humor comes from the situation, not from jokes told to loosen everyone up. If you say something stupid, or something that is obviously wrong, don't be afraid to admit it and laugh at yourself. Comedy comes from exaggeration and presenting the unexpected. If something goes awry, acknowledge it and move on.

Power structures are tricky in business. Most managers are willing to listen to the people on their teams, but on occasion, you'll find managers who just want things done the way they said. In extreme cases, managers might not be willing to admit that the approach they settled on won't actually work. Admitting when you're wrong and adjusting accordingly are valuable skills that managers should learn. The earlier that lesson's learned, the better.

Having a power structure in an improv group might seem like a contradiction in terms. After all, you're just making it up as you go along right? Actually no. Most improv groups have one or more directors. The main group that I play with has a general manager and an artistic director. The general manager's the owner, so of course whatever he says goes, but the artistic director has the power to make decisions about the show. I disagree with some of the decisions the artistic director has made, but if I created the show that I wanted to see, no one else would come. It is very important to understand your limitations.

New improv groups, especially those that try to rule by consensus, often run into problems when there are differences of opinion. Often a group of four or five people get together because they enjoy playing as a team. After a few shows or a few months, it's highly likely that some differences will come up regarding the show and the group's direction. If there is a strong director, they can make decisions on casting based on individuals that they feel will buy into the overall concept. It's a lot like hiring for a project team, but it's easier to get rid of people.

The last issue, resolving issues without forcing consensus, is troublesome, unless you have a hierarchy in place within which people are empowered to make a final decision on direction and method. At Intel, there is something called the *plan of record*, usually referred to as the POR. The idea is that all work must conform to the POR. One director at the company insisted that work follow the plan, even if everyone knew the POR was going to change. "The plan is the plan," he would say. In a way, the POR became the consensus vision once it was adopted.

The real benefit of having a plan is that you can have progress even without full consensus. You can feel free to disagree as long as you keep working and making progress on your aspect of the project without affecting the coherence of the team. Improv groups are specifically susceptible to this sort of disagreement because everyone feels like they have a significant stake in what's going on. They do, but in many cases it's better for a disgruntled individual to form their own team with their goals in mind.

When Consensus Goes Wrong

It might seem that not moving forward until your group achieves consensus is a good thing. In fact, Eisenhardt, Kahwajy, and Bourgois found that the forcing consensus actually had negative impacts. They stated:

> People usually associate consensus with harmony, but we often found the opposite: teams that insisted on resolving substantive conflict by forcing consensus tended to display the most interpersonal conflict.

It's easy to see why groups that insist on consensus have conflicts. The stakes are extremely high on a personal level – everyone wants to be right, and disagreement creates internal pressure that gets released in unproductive ways.

But let's suppose that everyone does agree. Having everyone on the same page is a good thing, right? Not always. It is possible to take consensus and conformity too far. The best example of what can happen when a group's consensus becomes pathological comes from the work of Irving Janis.

In his book *Groupthink*, Janis identifies eight symptoms that may indicate the presence of too much conformity:

- An illusion of invulnerability, shared by all or most of the members, which creates excessive optimism and encourages the group to take extreme risks.

- An unquestioned belief in the group's inherent morality, inclining members to ignore the ethical or moral consequences of their decisions.

- Collective efforts to rationalize in order to discount warnings or other information that might lead members to reconsider their assumptions.

- Stereotyped views of the enemy or competition, portraying them as evil, weak, or stupid.

- Self-censorship of deviations from the apparent group consensus

- A shared illusion of unanimity that puts tremendous pressure on individual group members to conform to the majority view

- Direct pressure on any member who expresses arguments against the group's assumptions, illusions, or commitments

- Self-appointed mind guards who act as a group to bring dissenting members into conformity with the group's or leader's position.

You can probably think of plenty of examples of businesses or other groups that have developed this dysfunctional level of consensus and conformity. I can come up with several examples of improv groups that thought their particular approach was superior to all others. Obviously, there is no such thing. What you do depends on your group's skills and the wants and needs of your audience. In fact, if you're a member of several different groups, you'll probably have different philosophies for each one.

I won't go point by point through Janis's list, but I do want to highlight the third item: collective efforts to rationalize in order to discount warnings or other information that might lead members to reconsider their assumptions. We all try to bring information from the world into our existing model so we can make sense of it within our own, framework. Problems arise when we twist that information so it fits what we already believe. It is possible that some of our most deeply held beliefs about the world, either from a business or artistic standpoint, do not fit the facts of our environment. Perhaps they once did, or perhaps they will in the future, but it's also possible that we have allowed our preferences to blind us to what's really out there. Watch out for this sort of rationalization. Those are early warning signs that a groupthink incident might be in progress.

I highly recommend Janis's book *Groupthink*. It's a classic treatise that often gets summarized in the eight points I listed above, but the entire book contains valuable insights and you would do yourself a great service by reading it through at least once.

Keeping Your Team Creative
Teresa M. Amibile has some very interesting ideas on how to kill creativity. She argues that there are three components of

creativity: expertise, creative thinking, and motivation. She believes that there is an intrinsic motivation principle of creativity: that people will be most creative when they feel motivated primarily by the interest, satisfaction, and challenge of the work itself – and not by external pressures. As the author of the Dale Carnegie Training book *The 5 Essential People Skills* points out: rewards encourage people to focus narrowly on a task, to do it as quickly as possible, and to take fewer risks. You maximize your personal rewards by doing what you get paid for. If you get a bonus for shipping software by a particular date, you will move heaven and earth to get it approved and shipped by that date.

The problem with this approach is what management experts called *suboptimization*. Rather than have the overall goal of a great product in mind, the manager could suboptimize by shipping whatever is available rather than what is good for the customer. Microsoft tries to avoid this trap by announcing that something will ship "when it's ready." It's not until the next version of Windows or Office is well along that the company will announce the next step in the testing and release sequence.

You can also find suboptimization in the theater world. In an improv context, players might go on stage with the goal of playing a great character in the next scene. They could then spend so much time concentrating on the character that they forget to honor the offers made by their fellow players.

Amibile names six general categories of managerial practices that affect creativity: challenge, freedom, resources, work group features, supervisory encouragement, and organizational support. What I find particularly insightful, however, is her take on how to stimulate creativity.

Perhaps the most efficacious way to stimulate creativity is to match people with the right assignments. Managers can match people with jobs that play to their expertise and their skills and creative thinking, and ignite intrinsic motivation. Perfect matches stretch employees' abilities. The amount of stretch, however, is crucial: not so little that they feel bored, but not so much that they feel overwhelmed and threatened by a loss of control.

Sometimes you have to assign someone to do the grunt work, but when you can, you should always give them assignments that allow them to spread their wings, use their current abilities to their fullest, and develop new skills.

7

Creating and Evaluating Performances

I have spent a lot of time describing the skills that you need for a successful improv performance. Through no small coincidence, they are also the skills that you need for a successful business operation.

There is no magic formula that tells you how to prepare and perform in every possible situation. No process is foolproof; most are, at best, fool-resistant. Even so, after you have prepared and turned your improvisational brainstorming into a scripted and hopefully rehearsed performance, there is nothing left to do but put it out there for your audience.

Without that performance, any preparations you go through will be meaningless. Basarab Nicolescu, a Romanian theatrical trainer, noted that:

> So exercises and improvisations have little particular value in themselves, but they facilitate a tuning of the theatrical 'instrument' that is the actor's being, and a circulation of 'living dramatic flow' in the actors as a group. The theatrical 'miracle' is produced afterwards, in the active presence of the audience, when an opening towards the 'unknown' can be mobilised more fully.

Improv performances can sometimes be difficult to judge. Laughter is almost always a good sign if you're doing comedy, but it's not the only valid reaction. Your audience could be paying attention to the story and enjoying it without necessarily finding it humorous enough to laugh. It's also possible that they aren't enjoying your performance at all. Regardless, it is important that you not delude yourself into thinking the latter reaction is actually the first.

One of the best ways to judge the success of an improv performance, or any performance for that matter, is to have one or more colleagues in the audience so they can tell you how the audience's energy changed during your presentation. For improv, you might also consider having a camera focused on the audience instead of on the stage. That way, when you watch the video later, you can hear what was happening on stage, but still focus on the audience reaction. If they're silent because they're checking their phones, drifting off to sleep, or consulting briefly with their seatmate about whether to make their escape, it would be reasonable to assume that your performance was not well received.

In a business context, it always helps to have a colleague sit with you, facing your audience. Just like the video camera for an improv group, your colleague can closely monitor the audience to see how they are reacting. Even if they can't help you during your presentation, they will be able to give you feedback both on your delivery and the structure of your presentation.

After you start performing, you need to adapt to whatever happens. Improvisational thinking will help this. After a time, you will find that you are less distracted by deviations from the path. Interestingly, you'll find that the more you rehearse your presentation, the easier it will be for you to get back on track in case you're distracted.

Knowing exactly what you want to say next is crucial to the success of any performance – business or theatrical. Sanford Meisner, an acting coach and director, developed the Meisner technique for actors developing a character within a scripted piece. The first step is to memorize the script so you can repeat it quickly without giving any inflection to the lines. You just want to regurgitate what is written on the page.

When you give a presentation for the first time, you need to trust in your preparations, which should include a warm-up of that isn't directly connected to the presentation. Merely going over the words and presentation keeps you locked in and concentrating, but gives your subconscious no time to consolidate your thoughts.

I know it's not always possible to warm up effectively before a presentation, especially at the last minute. If you've prepared properly, though, you will find that your presentation will flow smoothly and that you will be able to adapt to whatever happens. Remember that you and the other members of the group should have the best interests of your organization at heart. Your presentation should focus on that aspect as well as providing details on how following your proposed plan will benefit the individuals in the room.

Improv techniques can help you deal with users more effectively. Rather than try to break down exactly why someone reacted the way they did, you acknowledge their response and reply in a way that encourages more insight. You can always review the performance later.

Telling an Effective Story
With those considerations in mind, the question becomes how do you create a successful business presentation? If you want

to use PowerPoint slides, I recommend Cliff Atkinson's *Beyond Bullet Points*. He is a fellow Microsoft Press author, and his book, which is now in its third edition, sells in enviable quantities. I like his method for developing business presentations, especially if you only have a few minutes to talk, but there are other methodologies you can use to shape the words you say.

I've hinted at ways to create an effective story, both individually and as part of a team, but I'll go into more detail to emphasize techniques of effective storytelling.

Stephen Denning, formerly director of knowledge management at the World Bank, argues that a story told in a business context should be different from the story told in a theatrical or storytelling context. Storytellers adhere to the classical Aristotelian structure:

Act 1: Chase your hero up a tree.

Act 2: Throw rocks at him.

Act 3: Let him down.

This approach works well for improvised theater, but it is less well suited to a modern business presentation.

The biggest problem is that decision-makers suppress their emotions. They want hard facts and analysis that will allow them to justify their decisions. Denning argues that the objective approach lets decision-makers cut through the fog of salesmanship and focus on what truly matters. Of course, he also points out that:

> [T]his strength is also weakness. Analysis might excite the mind, but hardly offers a route to the

heart. And that's where you must go if you're to motivate people not only to take action but to do so with energy and enthusiasm.

The trick to effective storytelling is to find the proper balance between analytical thinking and rhetorical persuasion. Denning further notes that senior decision-makers have very little time to listen to a fleshed-out narrative. Instead, he advises that you take 30 to 60 seconds at the beginning of the presentation to communicate your vision for your project's outcome, and how it will benefit the people in the room. Your goal is to have your audience start to tell the story along with you, filling in details you don't have time to provide. As they become invested in creating the story, they will start to feel a sense of ownership in your narrative and will be more likely to provide their support.

As you're speaking, pay attention to your audience's reaction. It can be difficult to split your attention between what you're saying and your audience, but that's another area where rehearsal comes in handy. The more you have internalized your message, the more mental bandwidth you have open to keep in touch with your audience.

You can use the String of Pearls exercise described in the Appendix to create, rehearse, and deliver your presentations as a story.

Mick Napier, a long-time improviser who founded and directs the Annoyance Theatre in Chicago, offers this advice in his book *Improvise: Scene from the Inside Out*:

- Practice identifying the dominant energy.

- Practice responding to and acknowledging that energy while staying true to your own initiation at the beginning of the scene

I highly recommend Stephen Denning's books, which I have listed in the bibliography. They are terrific resources and present his personal story of how he overcame substantial resistance within the World Bank to create his knowledge management program. Napier's book is a thin, highly focused volume that gets to the heart of improvisation. Whether you're an improviser or a business person with no performing experience, he offers a variety of advice you can use to inform your presentations and other interactions.

Postmortem Analysis

Once you've completed your presentation, whether in a conference room or on stage, you pack up and go home. As soon as your audience departs, you should start discussing your performance with your colleagues. If it's just you, you might use your mobile phone to record voice notes to yourself.

The military term for analyzing mission performance is an *after action review*, or a *hot wash-up*. This is the time to bring up every little thing that went well, that went as expected, or that could've been improved. The idea isn't to humiliate or venerate the participants, but instead to provide an objective analysis of the preparation, delivery, and reaction to the presentation. Everybody has an ego. It's important both to protect it and to keep it in check.

During performance reviews, everyone should be completely honest about what they felt and listen carefully while other team members speak. This is not a time to go on a rant or indulge in an "I-told-you-so" moment. While emptions are high, it is best to listen.

Ken Weber, a longtime entertainer and now head of a successful investment advisory firm in New York, wrote the book *Maximum Entertainment*. In that book, he argues the time you spend driving back from a gig is the best time to review your performance. That's when the observations will flow freely because you can remember more about what happened and how you reacted to it. His advice: Keep the radio turned off until you have fully reviewed what you just did.

Premortems

Anytime you advocate change, you should expect to encounter resistance. There are, after all, vested interests in maintaining the status quo. That's as true for improv groups as it is for any other type of organization. One way you can reduce the disruption caused by these objections is to anticipate them and prepare responses.

To anticipate these problems, you can do a *premortem* where you probe a plan for every possible point of weakness. This is where you can release your negativity: Think of every possible way someone could object to your plan, how things could go wrong, whether your assumptions could be called into question, and whether the projected benefits are realistic.

There are two benefits to this exercise. The first, as I mentioned, is that you anticipate potential problems and can develop responses. If you can't develop a good answer to an objection, perhaps you should put off your presentation. The second benefit is that it helps detach team members from the proposal on an emotional level. Once you think of all the ways something could go wrong, you are much less likely to see it as a perfect plan. Doing so lets you receive criticism objectively, and answer without your emotions taking hold.

Remember that decision-makers prefer to operate on an analytical level, even when they are selling products or political candidates to their target demographic on pure emotion. If you present your analysis and let your persuasive techniques season what you say, you'll be that much closer to making your plan a reality.

8

My Favorite Improv Book by a Non-Improviser

Creative individuals of all types, but especially improvisers, must draw inspiration from multiple sources. Painters visit museums to view other paintings, but they also look at sculpture, pay attention to the clothes and hairstyles of other patrons, and observe the scenery as they walk to and from their hotel, subway stop, or car. Writers listen to others' stories so they can adapt what they hear for their own use. It's the whole premise of Austin Kleon's book, *Steal Like an Artist*, which I recommend highly.

The difference between improvisers and other artists is that unless they choose to accept a commission, other artists get to select their subject. Improvisers can decide whether to show up, what sort of suggestions to get, and how to shape what the audience gives them. It sounds like improvisers have a lot of control and, in a sense, we do, but we still allow the audience enormous influence over our creations.

Where do improvisers turn for inspiration? Everywhere.

Improvisers read websites for *CNN*, *ESPN*, and (spirits preserve us) the celebrity cyber-rag *TMZ* to learn about people, events, and issues our audience might shout out. We can't afford to ignore the parts of our popular culture that we hate. For example, reality television makes my teeth hurt. I watch as little of it as I can, but even I know that Boston Rob is a successful contestant on *Survivor*, not a corned beef sandwich served in Commonwealth Avenue delicatessens.

You have no idea how much I hope readers will have to look up that reference. A man can dream.

My current favorite improv book by a non-improviser is Matthew Frederick's *101 Things I Learned in Architecture School*. Frederick distilled the wisdom he's developed over his career as an architect, urban designer, and instructor into 101 aphorisms meant to help burgeoning architects deal with the rigors of their undergraduate training and develop a viable creative process. As it turns out, most of his advice applies directly to improvisational comedy and to the business world.

Architecting Improv

After noting that architectural design springs from an idea, Frederick states that "the more specific a design idea is, the greater its appeal is likely to be." His example shows two churches, one that represents itself as being for everyone and the other for purple-striped vegetarians. The church that's targeted at a very specific group is much better attended than the other generic church.

Improv scenes are based on *offers*, which are scene details that arise from player's statement or action. An offer, such as walking through a door, stamping one's feet, and then taking off earmuffs, coat, and gloves tells us that the character just came in from the snow. The player's emotion and intention can give even more information. If she moves quickly and yanks off her hat, it might mean that it is bitter cold outside. If she moves slowly and sets down her purse before taking off her cold weather gear, she might have trudged for half a mile through foot-deep drifts because the bus was on a snow route and couldn't get up her hill.

Frederick's nineteenth dictum states that one should start a composition with general elements and add details once the outline has been drawn. This fits well within the context of improvised theatre but does have its limitations. The offer I just described provides details but doesn't drive the scene in any particular direction. This kind of offer gives the second player a lot of room to work. He could open a window, for example, signaling a conflict between his perception of the room as too hot and the first performer's obvious chill.

The author also notes that aesthetic qualities are enhanced by the presence of counterpoint. In music, *counterpoint* is the combination of multiple melodies. If you use the term as a verb, it means to clarify or heighten something by juxtaposing or contrasting it with something else. Improvisers typically use the term *conflict* to describe the technique used to shove a situation off balance and generate action. Unfortunately, the word conflict, when used in the general sense, connotes a fight or struggle between two or more incompatible outlooks. And, yes, that is what's going on in the action of the scene, but it's easy to take the competitive aspect too far and kill your forward momentum through an unwillingness to compromise.

Which brings me to another of Frederick's points: A good designer isn't afraid to throw out a good idea. Architects are paid to have good ideas, and the skillful ones generate them quickly when they're working well. The problem isn't that a good designer won't have enough good ideas—the problem is that he usually has too many and will run aground trying to jam all of them into the same project.

The same concern holds for improvisers. We're trained to react to what's happening on stage and to make offers that both heighten the action and take the scene in a worthwhile direction. I love it when another performer tells me that a choice I made gave them a springboard to move the scene forward. By the same token, I have to realize that when there are four people on stage, any one of us could make the offer that propels the scene forward. The trick is to realize when that foundation offer has been made, take advantage of it, and give your fellow player the credit after the show.

Of course, "throwing out" a good idea doesn't mean forgetting it entirely—it just means that you don't use it immediately. Everyone learns from experience and adds unused material to their toolkit. Piers Anthony, a Young Adult science fiction and fantasy writer, programmed a series of commands into his word processor that let him record ideas in a separate document as they occurred to him. He could then examine those ideas between projects or when he needed inspiration for his current work. Note pads, voice memos, and e-mails to yourself all serve the same purpose.

Regardless of the method, try to maintain a central log of your unused ideas and revisit the collection occasionally. I tend to write my ideas in spiral-bound graph paper notebooks. When I consolidated several years of notes a few months ago, I realized I'd come up with the same idea four times. That sort of repetition is embarrassing, but it's better than not having the idea at all.

Frederick also points out that the most effective architects examine their design processes through meta-thinking, or "thinking about the thinking." Performers of all kinds spend hours working with directors who offer encouragement, advice, and techniques to help them hone their skills. Newer performers are like teenagers just learning to drive—they concentrate on so many details and encounter so many situations for the first time that their driving is rough, choppy, and almost entirely without flow. With time, however, improvisers assimilate the basics into their unconscious.

That's not to say that learning new things is easy. Every time an improviser tries to learn a new skill, he or she goes through the same process of fumbling through their workshops and performances until the new approach becomes part of their unconscious. Chess players go through the same process whenever they try to improve. Adding a new opening to one's repertoire, developing techniques for converting a winning position into a won game, and recognizing transitions within a game are all skills that change your outlook on chess and affect your game. Most often, these changes hurt your game in the short term—when you look at the board, your ingrained habits fight for supremacy with your new outlook, and you're caught between the two approaches. Golfers, tennis players, and other athletes report the same issues. Eventually, they either succeed at integrating the new approach or return to their old patterns and seek other ways to improve.

Who's in Control?

Kinesthesiologists refer to walking as "controlled falling." To move forward, you must first unbalance your body and then catch yourself before you hit the ground. This basic human activity illustrates our lives perfectly. Not only must we create an imbalance to make progress; we have to do so repeatedly. Human existence is about the struggle to control one's environment. Whether you arrange your work area so you're comfortable or you go after a job, you think will make you happy, you're fighting for control.

Improv groups relying on a single individual can do good work, but in many cases the group's performances will be something less than the sum of its parts. As Frederick points out, "properly gaining control of the design process tends to feel like one is losing control of the design process." In another context, racing great Mario Andretti said, "If everything seems under control, you're not going fast enough."

Improv teams are just like other groups in that everyone is responsible for everyone else's success. When a performer makes a choice on stage, it is everyone's job to make that choice work. In relation to architectural design, Frederick says that every choice must be justified in at least two ways. In improv, *justification* means incorporating an offer into a scene. There are times when players make multiple offers and only one can be used, or someone makes an offer that can't be incorporated without wrecking the scene. Among experienced players those incidents are exceedingly rare. Yes, you always want to make great offers, but Frederick argues that a beautiful composition is the result of a harmonious relationship among the design elements, not a grouping of the most beautiful elements available.

Finally, Frederick points out that limitations encourage creativity. Some improvisers, particularly younger ones, want to perform with either no or minimal constraints on their creation. For them, true improvisation isn't constrained by suggestions or game rules. Instead, they might not even get a suggestion before starting …something… based on whatever comes to mind. This type of production can work, but the process relegates the audience to the role of passive observers. As I've said several times before: if audience members expect to see improvised theatre but have no chance to affect the performance, how do they know what they're seeing is truly improvised?

Like architects who work within the constraints of space, budget, client desires, and the laws of physics, improvisers should strongly consider ceding more control to their audience. Stepping out of the constraints imposed by high school and college instructors and spreading one's wings feels wonderful to the performer, but it's not as satisfying for audience members who expect to participate in the process. Rehearsals, workshops, and performances for other improvisers present wonderful opportunities to work from scratch and indulge. That said, I argue that paying audiences deserve the chance to play their role, too.

What Did Frederick Leave Out?

One lesson I wish had made it into *101 Things I Learned in Architecture School* is that different phases of a project require different skills and behaviors. For architects, the initial planning stage requires intense listening so you understand what the client wants. After you know your goal, you think imaginatively and use your repertoire of design skills to create a solution that meets your client's goals while staying within the project's physical and budgetary constraints. Once construction starts, you need to answer questions, clarify goals, and be ready to resolve any problems that come up. Finally, as the project nears completion, architects must verify the work that's been done and help bring the development to a successful close.

Like architects, improvisers use different skills as a scene or game progresses. At the start of the performance, the players decide which games they're going to play (possibly with the help of the audience) and get one or more suggestions. Then the players create their work based on their client's (the audience) guidance. One or more players then initiate the scene, and the other players jump in or stay on the side as required entertain. Every player must maintain a careful watch on the scene's action and time constraints to ensure that the plot moves forward and that the scene's action will resolve, or at least come to a point at which the scene can be halted, to fit the game and show's length requirements.

Some players are marvelous at scene initiations, whereas others specialize at being the "third player in," taking what's been created and adding to the scene with a contribution that honors what has gone before and pushes the scene to new heights. I think of myself as a player who knows how to keep the plot moving forward in a narrative game, such as a musical comedy, or a long-form show such as an improvised play in the style of Shakespeare in which multiple plot lines need to be resolved.

As with architects, improvisers do best when they practice and perform as often as possible, when they listen to feedback both during and after the work process, and think about what they've done and how they can build on their successes and correct their shortcomings.

9

Some Final Words

I've spent the last 20 years of my life as a professional improvisational comedian. The early years were rough. I had many habits and outlooks that didn't mesh with an art form that required significant cooperation. I overcame many of those blocks over time, but there's always work to be done.

I hope I've demonstrated how rich and varied improvisation can be as an art form. For the uninitiated, improv performances look like a bunch of people having fun on stage. In many ways, that's exactly right. Then, on further reflection, audience members wonder how it can all happen so quickly and reliably.

It's also possible for improv performances to go horribly, terribly wrong. Sometimes, for what seems like no discernible reason, a team that warmed up well and is in good spirits steps on stage and delivers a flat, uninspired performance. That's why some groups aren't willing to risk failure. Rather than take a chance that a performance won't work, they claim to do improv when they're actually doing scripted sketch comedy.

You might have been surprised to find a chapter on game theory in a book on applying improv comedy to business. Feel free to blame my nerdish nature—there are times when everything I see looks like math. That said, I most emphatically do not believe that performance, or personal relationships of any kind, should be broken down into precise equations. Of course, it's possible to find and share best practices you and your colleagues have developed through years of experience, but it's the unexpected nature of what we do that makes the journey so thrilling for us and so joyful.

I don't want to claim too much for my own admitted preference. As much as I enjoy improv, it's not for everyone, and it's certainly not appropriate for every situation. Many business interactions, particularly in the technical support realm, should be templated, if not scripted in part. That said, the second you step outside these carefully controlled settings, improv comes into play. There will be times when I'm making it up as I go along and trying desperately to find a thread that lets me drag the situation back onto familiar ground.

In closing, there are seven things I hope you take away from reading *Improspectives*:

- Make strong choices so you and your team can move forward.

- Do not require an artificial consensus before moving forward.

- Use the "Yes, and…" principle to facilitate brainstorming and problem-solving.

- Listen carefully and ask questions so you don't have to read anyone's mind.

- Try to identify your beliefs and biases so you understand how you process information about the world.

- Take a page from the Tit for Tat program that won Axelrod's Prisoner's Dilemma tournament: Be nice, provokable, forgiving, and transparent.

- Expand your horizons beyond your current work and social environment. Travel where you can and read as much as you can about a wide variety of subjects.

I hope you enjoyed reading *Improspectives* as much as I enjoyed writing it. To continue this conversation, please visit *www.improspectives.com*.

Appendix

One of the hallmarks of all theatre, especially improv, is that the players warm up together before a show. Often these warm-ups include a physical game or two to increase the players' energy, a verbal game to get everyone used to talking, and a teamwork or concentration game to get everyone ready to work together.

Every team is different, so I've provided several games you should consider using to help your team start thinking and working together. You'll find games that help you find out more about each other, get your blood flowing and energy up, help you tell stories, and brainstorm effectively.

I want to emphasize that these games are fun to play and that there are no winners or losers. They work best when you move quickly, which means that players will make mistakes. That's OK—you're supposed to make mistakes. In fact, if you're playing the game too well, you need to speed up.

When someone messes up, you should have a brief ritual: acknowledge the mistake and then have that person start the next round of the game. If you're in a circle, one possible ritual is to throw your arms around your neighbors' shoulders, take one small step forward, and say "Whatever" in unison.

Performing this little ritual releases the tension while acknowledging something went awry. Then, with the mistake behind you, you can move forward.

Line-Ups

Type
Teambuilding

Description
In the game of Line-Ups, the players arrange themselves in a line according to some criteria. The players can't speak while they maneuver into position. Once in position, the leader can let everyone talk to determine whether they should change places.

Variations
Players can line up by height, age, or hair color.

Other choices include lining up by the day of the month the players were born on, the distance of their commute, or the first letter of their favorite hobby.

Add a second dimension to make a square and give two choices, such as how much they enjoy reading and how much they enjoy watching movies.

Goal
The goal of this game is to let the participants get more familiar with each other and to get used to moving around without communicating.

Everybody Who

Type
Teambuilding

Description
In the game of Everybody Who, there is one fewer chair than there are participants, and everyone sits except for one participant. The person who is standing says something truthful about himself. Everyone for whom that statement is also true must stand up and move to another chair (that is, they can't return to the chair they got up from.) The participant left standing continues the game by saying something truthful about himself or herself.

Variations
Players can't move to a chair next to their original chair.

Anyone who says something that is true of exactly one other person gets a huge round of applause.

Goal
The goal of this game is to let the participants get more familiar with each other and to learn to move from chair to chair without violence.

Something in Common

Type
Teambuilding

Description
In the game of Something in Common, the participants divide into groups of three. Their task is to find something in common, other than the obvious, such as working for the same company, attending the same function, or being the same gender.

Variations
Expand the groups to include more members.

Require the "thing in common" to be something fairly specific. "I was born in the spring" could become "I was born in April", for example.

Goal
The goal of this game is to let the participants get more familiar with each other and to work toward finding common ground.

Zip-Zap-Zop

Type
Speed and energy

Description
In the game of Zip-Zap-Zop, the participants pass an "it" around the circle. The first player says *zip* and points at another player, who is now "it". The second player points at someone else and says *zap*. The third player points at another player and says *zop*. The player that receives the *zop* restarts the pattern with a *zip*.

Variations
The first player pointed to, instead of staying *zap*, can pass a second *zip* to another player. The new "it" can then pass a *zap* or another *zip*. However many *zips* are passed, that is the number of *zaps* and *zops* that must be said during that round. In other words, if the first three moves are *zip-zip-zap*, the next player must say *zap* to continue the pattern.

A player who is "it" can point to two players simultaneously, splitting the "it" into two paths.

A very advanced variation is to make up three hand signals and play the game silently.

Goal
The goal of this game is to move at a fast pace to get your energy up.

Zoom Schwartz

Type
Speed and energy

Description

In the game of Zoom Schwartz, the participants pass an "it" around the circle. There are three basic rules: *zoom, schwartz,* and *pafigliano.*

- *Zoom* sends the "it" to any other player in the circle.

- *Schwartz* sends the "it" back to the person who just sent it.

- *Pafigliano* sends the "it" to the person to the active player's immediate left or right.

Variations

You can add new rules to the game. Two other rules you could add are:

- You Can't Zoom a Zoom: As the rule implies, you can't respond to a zoom with another zoom.

- Murph: Say *murph*, then throw your hands in the air and say "Ahhh!" You may then make any available move.

Goal

The goal of this game is to move at a fast pace to get your energy up.

Last Letter, First Letter

Type
Listening

Description
In the game of Last Letter, First Letter, players assemble in pairs. The first player asks a question, to which the second player responds with a sentence that begins with the last letter of the question. For example:

Player 1:   Where did you go on vacatio<u>n</u>?

Player 2:   <u>N</u>orth Carolina. Have you ever been the<u>re</u>?

Player 1:   <u>E</u>very year we visit my wife's family in Raleigh.

Variations
Try starting each statement with the next letter in the alphabet. For example:

Player 1:   <u>A</u>re you going to Mexico this year?

Player 2:   <u>B</u>elieve it or not, we've already been.

Player 1:   <u>C</u>ancun, or Puerto Vallarta?

Goal
The goal of this game is to listen to everything the other player says and incorporate it into your response.

Categories

Type
Brainstorming

Description
In the game of Categories, someone names a broad category, such as breeds of cat. The players take turns naming items in that category until someone responds too slowly or repeats something said before. When that happens, the player names a new category and the game continues.

Variations
Give a player a category and have her name seven things in that category.

Send a player out of the room and agree on a category. When the player comes back, give examples of things in that category and see if he can guess the category.

Goal
The goal of this game is to get your brain used to coming up with items in response to suggestions.

Counting

Type
Concentration

Description
In the game of Counting, the players form a tight circle and close their eyes. The players then start counting aloud from the number one. If any players speak at the same time, the group must start over.

Variations
Count by some increment other than one. Seven sounds easy, but it can be difficult.

Count to a target number and then start counting backward.

Goal
The goal of this game is to encourage sharing and help players sense when it's their turn to act.

Pass the Clap

Concentration

Description
In the game of Pass the Clap, the team forms a circle and selects someone to start. The starter faces one of their neighbors and they clap at the same time. It's harder than it sounds, but the key is to make good, solid eye contact. The second player then turns to the other neighbor and they clap at the same time. Continue around the circle and try to maintain a constant beat without speeding up.

Variations
Add a second clap (and third, and fourth) after the first clap has gone around a few times.

Speed up to make the game harder.

Goal
The goals of this game are to concentrate on a seemingly simple action (clapping in unison) and to switch from one task to another when there are multiple actions.

Word at a Time Story

Type
Narrative

Description
In the game of Word at a Time Story, the players go around the circle telling a story one word at a time.

Variations
Allow each player to say two words, three words, or some other exact number.

Instead of going around the circle, the player who just spoke can point to another player.

Goal
The goal of this game is to move at a fast pace while maintaining a reasonably coherent story. Players also get used to limiting their input and allowing other players to influence the story.

Sentences of X Words

Type
Narrative

Description
In the game of Sentences of X Words, pairs of players act in a scene in which every sentence must have a specific number of words.

Variations
Change the number of words allowed for each sentence.

Let the player combine words and physical actions to meet the target number of "words."

Goal
The goal of this game is to move at a fast pace while maintaining a reasonably coherent story. Players also get used to limiting their input and allowing other players to influence the story.

String of Pearls

Narrative

Description
In the game of String of Pearls, the first player establishes the first plot point of a story. The second player establishes the last plot point of a story. The other players fill in the middle of the story in any order.

Variations
Have all players go in order, starting with the first plot point and ending with the last.

Have the players name the plot points in reverse order.

Goal
The goal of this game is to establish a coherent narrative.

Tableaux

Narrative

Description
In the game of Tableaux, a team of three or four players create a series of three physical positions that represent the start, middle, and end of a scene. No player can talk or direct any other player while forming the positions. The team then plays the scene, starting with the first position, including the second position in the middle of the scene, and ending the scene with the final position.

Variations
Have the players create the positions in reverse order.

Leave one player out of each position and let them join each position as a wildcard.

Goal
The goal of this game is to establish a coherent narrative.

Layups

Type
Narrative

Description
In the game of Layups, the team forms two lines and the first two players step forward. One player says a single sentence that initiates a scene without asking a question or starting an argument. The other player responds with something that affirms what the other player said and adds to it. For example:

Player 1:   I've always loved that sweater.

Player 2:   Thanks! My wife bought it for me on our first ski trip.

Variations
Require the first player to establish the "who" of the scene by naming the other player and hinting at their relationship.

Require the second player to establish the "where" of the scene by indicating the physical location.

Extend the scene to three or more lines.

Ask the players to repeat the lines in reverse order.

Goal
The goal of this game is to establish a firm footing for a scene, reinforce the need for agreement within the scene, and to require the players to remember what was said.

Tricorder

Type
Milieu exploration

Description
In the game of Tricorder, a group of four or five players take on roles from the original Star Trek series. The "Away Team" usually includes a command officer, science officer, medical officer, and security officer. Players take turns getting "readings" off their tricorder and describe what they see.

Variations
Expand the character types to any television series.

Instead of science fiction, set the scene in another genre such as fantasy or horror.

Allow each character to ask questions of others after everyone has given their initial report.

Goal
The goal of this game is to let the participants stretch their imaginations and to describe what they see so their teammates can understand exactly what the speaker is experiencing.

Works Consulted

Axelrod, Robert. The *Evolution of Cooperation*. New York: Basic Books, 1984.

Dale Carnegie Training. *The 5 Essential People Skills*. New York: Simon & Schuster, 2009.

Denning, Stephen. *The Leader's Guide to Storytelling*. San Francisco: John Wiley & Sons, 2005.

Denning, Stephen. *The Secret Language of Leadership*. San Francisco: John Wiley & Sons, 2007.

Denning, Stephen. *The Springboard: How Storytelling Ignites Action in Knowledge-Era Organizations*. Boston: Butterworth Heinemann, 2001.

Dixon, Nancy. *Common Knowledge: How Companies Thrive by Sharing What They Know*. Boston: Harvard Business School Press, 2000.

Frederick, Matthew. *101 Things I Learned in Architecture School*. Cambridge, MA: MIT Press, 2007.

Harvard Business Review. *Harvard Business Review on Breakthrough Thinking*. Boston: Harvard Business School Press, 1999.

Harvard Business Review. *Harvard Business Review on Effective Communication*. Boston: Harvard Business School Press, 1999.

Janis, Irving L. *Groupthink: Psychological Studies of Policy Decisions and Fiascoes*. Second edition, revised. Boston: Houghton Mifflin, 1983.

Klein, Gary. *Sources of Power: How People Make Decisions*. Cambridge, MA: MIT Press, 1999.

Kleon, Austin. *Steal Like an Artist*. New York: Workman Publishing, 2012.

Kline, John A. *Listening Effectively*: Achieving High Standards in Communication. Upper Saddle River, NJ: Pearson Education, 2003.

Langer, Ellen J. *Mindfulness*. Reading, MA: Addison-Wesley, 1989.

MacMillan, Pat. *The Performance Factor: Unlocking the Secrets of Teamwork*. Nashville, TN: Broadman & Holman, 2001.

Napier, Mick. *Improvise: Scene from the Inside Out*. Portsmouth, NH: Heinemann, 2004.

Roter, Debra L., and Judith A. Hall. *Doctors Talking with Patients/Patients Talking with Doctors*. Westport, CT: Auburn House, 1993.

Schrage, Michael. *Serious Play*. Boston: Harvard Business School Press, 2000.

Stevens, Scott P. *Games People Play: Game Theory in Life, Business, and Beyond*. Chantilly, VA: The Great Courses, 2008. DVD.

Index

Acknowledgments

Writing a book can be a solitary journey, but gaining the knowledge you put into it rarely is. For the last 20 years, I've been fortunate to work with a wide range of talented engineers, scientists, software developers, writers, editors, and improvisers. Many of my colleagues fit into several of those categories, which makes their perspectives that much more valuable.

In particular, I'd like to thank Patrick Short, General Manager of ComedySportz Portland, for giving my friends and me a home to pursue the art we love. I started pro-level workshops in February 1996 and still learn every time I go. Since taking over as artistic director, Andrew Berkowitz has helped us improve our performances and professionalism. To think that my improv journey started with the DC-based group Mprov back in 1993…

I'd also like to thank William A. Ruh (then of The MITRE Corporation), the gang at Microsoft Press for working with me on more than 20 books, and my agent Neil Salkind of Studio B and The Salkind Agency. During my writing career, I have been very fortunate to work with Nancy Sixsmith of ConText Editorial Services (*www.contextedit.com*) several times. I'm glad she was available to copy edit *Improspectives*.

Finally, I'd like to thank my family and friends who support me in my odd choice of career. Special thanks go to my wife Virginia, without whom none of this would mean anything.

About the Author

Curtis Frye is the author of more than two dozen books, including *Microsoft Excel 2013 Step by Step*, *Microsoft Excel 2013 Plain & Simple*, and *Privacy-Enhanced Business*. He graduated from Syracuse University with an honors degree in political science and started his professional career as a member of the technical staff at The MITRE Corporation in McLean, VA. During his time in the DC area, he performed with a local improv group.

After moving to Portland, Oregon, in 1995 to pursue his writing career, he joined ComedySportz Portland. Since then, he has performed in more than 1,100 shows with the professional cast. Curt also appears as a solo performer and keynote speaker. You can find out more about Curt at *www.curtisfrye.com* and continue the *Improspectives* conversation at *www.improspectives.com*.